THE JOE PUBLIC GUIDE TO
THE HISTORY OF ENGLAND

THE JOE PUBLIC GUIDE TO THE HISTORY OF ENGLAND

JOE CASTELLO

G2 RIGHTS LTD
KENT

First published 2009 by
Athena Press

Second Edition 2013 published by
G2 RIGHTS LTD.
Unit 7-8 Whiffens Farm, Clement Street,
Hextable, Kent BR8 7PQ
United Kingdom

ISBN 978-1-782810-45-2

Printed for G2 Rights Ltd.

The cost of producing this publication has been covered by
the generosity of our sponsors:

Jarvis Richardson
Jake Richardson
Arthur Reeve

As a result of their contributions, all royalties from this edition
will be donated to Diabetes UK.

CONTENTS

The Lancastrians

The Yorkists

The Tudors

The Stuarts

The Commonwealth

The Stuarts (restored)

The Hanovers

The Windsors

The royal houses and their order can be remembered by
the following aide-memoire:
No Plan Like Yours To Study History Wisely

Introduction

This book reduces 'The History of England' to a summary of headlines.

Its purpose is to give an overview and perspective of the main events.

It is also hoped to whet the reader's appetite for a greater knowledge than can be provided by this publication

This project combines school notes of the 1950s with a reread of *Our Island Story* by H E Marshall.

Wikipedia and *The British History Encyclopaedia* were used as references for the post-Victorian period.

The author took the position that any reign that commenced after his date of birth should be excluded, on the basis that it is current affairs rather than history!

Whatever any modern education theory may maintain, history is linear and vertical, and can only be understood in this way. Time may be an artificial construct, but it is the only one we have for understanding the past; and if you do not understand the past, you cannot understand the present. Once we have the vertical progression, then, indeed, we can branch off in a horizontal direction and then return to the main narrative. First get the facts. Of course the presentation here is simplistic; it has to be; but historical truth is simple.

There are, of course, some cynics who say that history is merely the propaganda of the victor.

Availability
This title, together with others in the Joe Public Guide series, are available via www.joepublicguide.com

The Romans

Brutus of Troy reputedly claimed the island, which he called Britain.

Many years later, in 55 BC, the Roman warrior, Julius Caesar, decided to cross from Gaul (France) so that he could add Britain to the Roman Empire.

He beat the ancient Britons a year later in battle but did not stay long in Britain.

Many of his ships were destroyed by storms. As a result Caesar did not leave any soldiers in Britain when he left.

In AD 43 Claudius invaded Britain. He beat the Britons who were lead by Caractacus. Caractacus and his family were taken to Rome as prisoners.

Resistance to the Roman occupation of Britain was then led by Queen Boadicea. She was Queen of the Iceni tribe which occupied what is now Norfolk and Suffolk.

They marched on the Romans and destroyed London and St Albans (Verulamium) after mass slaughter. After initial victories, the Britons were utterly defeated.

Boadicea poisoned herself and her children to death rather than face Roman slavery.

Then the Romans, under Julius Agricola, ruled Britain less oppressively.

Later, Emperor Hadrian ruled Britain. He built Hadrian's Wall across the North of England from the Tyne to the Solway in order to keep out the Picts and Scots.

The Romans taught the Britons about many useful things such as roads, building and education. In about AD 410 they left Britain altogether.

The ancient Britons were Pagans and worshipped the oak tree and mistletoe. The priests were called druids, who used human sacrifices. Gradually Christianity took over. The Christians were initially persecuted and the first Christian martyr in Britain was St Alban. He was put to death for renouncing the pagan religion. Verulamium then became St Albans.

The individuals named above, were dominant in the following order:

- Brutus of Troy
- Julius Caesar
- Claudius
- Boadicea
- Julius Agricola
- Hadrian

The Saxons

After the Romans left Britain, the Picts and Scots breached Hadrian's Wall and overran the country.

King Constantine drove them back to Scotland but was killed by a Pict. He was succeeded by his elder son, Constans. His much younger brothers were Aurelius Ambrosius and Uther Pendragon.

After a conspiracy, Constans was killed and replaced by Vortigern, who organised the conspiracy.

King Vortigern could not quell the Picts and Scots so he invited help from the Saxons of Germany. The first to arrive in AD 449 were led by Hengist and Horsa. They drove the Picts and Scots back to their own country.

Instead of going home, these Saxons decided to stay and conquer Britain for themselves.

King Vortigern then married Rowena, who was the daughter of Hengist. The marriage between a Briton and a Saxon was not popular.

Vortigern was driven from the throne and replaced by his son, Vortimer. Vortimer killed Horsa and drove Hengist back to Germany.

Rowena had Vortimer poisoned and Vortigern became king again.

Hengist and his men then returned to Britain and tricked the Britons into attending a big feast on Salisbury Plain while being unarmed. After a signal, the Saxons then slaughtered the Britons.

Hengist took possession of Britain. The Saxons swarmed over the country and caused havoc.

The Britons fled in terror to the mountains and forests.

At this point, the exiled brothers, Aurelius Ambrosius

and Uther Pendragon, collected an army and came sailing over from France to Britain. They wanted revenge on Vortigern for killing their brother Constans. Vortigern was killed in Wales. Vortigern was dead, but the Saxons whom he had brought to Britain were still the rulers of the land.

Aurelius and Uther marched against the Saxons, defeated them and executed Hengist. Aurelius became King of Britain and began to restore order. He was then poisoned by the Saxons.

Aurelius was succeeded by his brother, Uther Pendragon, who was also a good king. He spent most of his time fighting Saxons and was eventually poisoned by them.

Uther was then succeeded by the fifteen-year-old King Arthur who became one of the very best kings of Britain. He was determined to free his kingdom from the Saxons.

With his trusty sword called Excalibur, he fought and won twelve great battles against the Saxons.

And at last the Saxons were driven from the land. Then there were some years of peace. These were the days of Merlin the magician.

Rather than have his knights sit with him at a long table, where the seating position inferred favouritism, Arthur devised a round table, where there was neither a top nor bottom. Hence, King Arthur and the Knights of the Round Table.

The age of chivalry was shattered by a further invasion by the Saxons. This time Arthur and most of his knights were killed. The Saxons then totally dominated Britain. They came in greater and greater numbers as time went by. They were all Germanic people, but there were many different tribes among them. They included Angles and Jutes.

At last, most of the ancient Britons were killed off. The survivors took refuge in what is now Wales and Cornwall.

The people there are the descendants of the ancient Britons.

The Saxons divided the country into seven different kingdoms. They eventually became united under King Egbert, who was an Angle. He changed the name of the country from Britain to Angleland or England.

Egbert was the first King of England.

Having been Christian under Arthur, the land again became pagan. In AD 597, however, Augustine successfully brought Christianity back to England.

The individuals named above, were dominant in the following order:

- Constantine
- Constans
- Vortigern
- Hengist & Horsa
- Vortimer
- Vortigern
- Hengist
- Aurelius
- Uther Pendragon
- Arthur
- Egbert

The Danes and Vikings

Just as the Romans had come to conquer Britain, and as the Saxons themselves had followed after them, so now another people came across the sea. These invaders were Danes and Vikings from what is now Norway, Sweden and Denmark.

These pagan invaders began to dominate. They were then resisted and nearly driven out by the English king called Alfred.

Alfred was the grandson of Egbert, the first English king.

Alfred developed a navy to confront the Danes at sea before they arrived on English soil. In AD 875 he had a significant sea battle victory. England has had a Navy ever since.

The Danes went away but came back with a vengeance, defeated the English, and Alfred was forced to hide on an island in the marshes of Somerset. He concealed his identity and lived in the cottage of a swineherd.

It was here that Alfred plotted his successful fightback against the Danes.

After his victories and after crushing their power, Alfred made peace with the Danes.

His achievements in peacetime included setting out the 'Laws of the Land'. He introduced trial by jury. He rebuilt the monasteries destroyed by the Danes, and founded new schools.

He translated books from Latin into English. He built more ships and encouraged trade with other countries. This king became known as Alfred the Great. He died in about AD 901.

Over the next one hundred years there were many kings of England. These included Edward the Elder, with his sister Ethelfleda, Athelstane and Ethelred the Unready.

Over the same period, the Danes became more and more powerful. Increasing numbers settled in England but did not integrate. Others just came, looted and left. At one stage King Ethelred the Unready levied a tax called Danegeld. This money he offered to the Danes if they would leave England. They took the money and left, but returned quite soon. This process was repeated often.

As this plan had failed, Ethelred instigated a plan to slaughter by surprise all Danes living in England. On the predetermined date of 13 November 1002, all Danes were duly slaughtered. Among those killed was Princess Gunhilde, the sister of Sweyn, the King of Denmark. Sweyn's reaction was to bring a large army to totally ransack and destroy England. Ethelred fled to Normandy in France.

Before Sweyn could be crowned King of England, he died suddenly, leaving the throne to his son, Canute.

Ethelred then returned to claim England. He was a total coward and failed, despite the magnificent efforts of his son, Edmund Ironside.

Soon however, Ethelred died, and the people immediately crowned Edmund as king. Thus there became two kings of England, an English one and a Danish one. War between the two continued fiercely. Eventually they decided to fight in single combat. The loser would be buried like a king, and the winner would rule over all of England.

After a long fight without a decisive result, they decided to compromise and divide the country into two. Edmund Ironside ruled over the south part, and Canute took over the north. Sadly, Edmund died after a few months and Canute became King of all England. There was an agreement between them, that the survivor would take all.

As a precaution, Canute sent Edmund's two sons into exile in Hungary. He was now King of Norway, Sweden, Denmark and England! Although very powerful, he demonstrated to his fawning nobles that he did not have the power to reverse the tide. Canute became Christian and Christianity swept over England.

Under Canute, the difference between the Danes and the English began to pass away. They integrated and over a period of time became a united people.

Because he had other countries to rule, he divided England into four earldoms, and placed an earl over each part. These earls ruled the kingdom under Canute. The Earl of Wessex was a man named Godwin.

In 1035, King Canute died and was buried in the minster at Winchester.

The individuals name above, were dominant in the following order:

- Alfred
- Edward the Elder
- Athelstane
- Ethelred the Unready
- Sweyn
- Canute
- Edmund
- Canute

The Normans

The crown passed to King Canute's sons, Harold Harefoot and Hardicanute. When they died, Earl Godwin persuaded the English to crown Edward, the son of Ethelred the Unready. Edward was English but was raised in Normandy, where his father Ethelred fled to exile. He spoke Norman French and surrounded himself with Norman friends when he returned to England.

Godwin arranged for Edward to marry his daughter, Edith, in an effort to Anglicise him. The ploy failed.

Resentment and hatred increased between the English and the Normans.

Earl Godwin and his sons were banished to exile.

Queen Edith was put into a convent.

Edward's cousin, William of Normandy, visited England and made Edward promise that he should be the next king. Edward did so, even though he had no authority to do this.

Nearly all of the chief men at court were now Normans, and the people longed for Godwin and his sons to return to free them from these hated strangers. At last they did return. Edward was furious that they had disobeyed him, but nervous about how popular they were.

To preserve the peace, Godwin somehow persuaded the king to send all his Norman favourites back to France, and to use Englishmen instead. Peace was preserved.

Soon after this, Godwin died and his son Harold took his place. Edward was now old, so Harold effectively ruled England. He ruled well and banished his brother Tostig for ruling badly as the Earl of Northumbria. It then happened that Harold was shipwrecked off the coast of

Normandy and fell into the hands of Duke William of Normandy. He was imprisoned until he also promised to let William be King of England after Edward died. Harold made this promise, which he had no authority to make, in order to get out of prison.

In 1066 King Edward died and was buried at Westminster. He had become gentle and pious and was regarded as a holy man. Hence he became known as Edward the Confessor. His reign had been made more successful because of Godwin and his son Harold controlling his actions.

Harold Godwinson was chosen as king, even though he was not the heir to the throne. The rightful heir was a young boy who had spent all his life in Hungary. Harold was crowned in Westminster. The English were desperate for an English king.

In Rouen, when Duke William of Normandy heard that Harold had been crowned, he was livid with rage.

He sent a message to Harold to inform him that either he was to give up the throne peacefully, or that it would be taken by force. Harold replied that the people of England had put their trust in him and that he would protect them the best he could.

William's nobles were resistant to the idea of invading England until he bribed them with offers of considerable spoils of war.

He gathered a great army and fleet with which to invade England.

The individuals named above, were dominant in the following order:

- Harold Harefoot
- Hardicanute
- Edward the Confessor
- Harold Godwinson

William I 1066–1087

TWENTY-ONE YEARS

In January 1066, King Edward the Confessor died. The Witan (or Council) met, and chose Harold Godwin as King of England.

William of Normandy had a claim to the throne and so he decided to invade. The invasion was awaited all summer, but it never happened. Harold disbanded his army. Then a call from the North of England reported that 300 Norse longships under Harold Hardrada (the King of Norway) had arrived at the Humber.

Earl Tostig (Harold's brother) had invited him to take the throne. After many victories, they awaited Harold at Stamford Bridge, seven miles from York. During the battle, Harold Hardrada and Tostig were both killed, and the English won.

While this battle took place, William arrived unopposed on the Sussex shore.

Harold marched hard from York to Sussex. His army was reduced in size and very tired. He should have rested and waited for reinforcements; however, with his hot temper he joined battle at Senlac Hill. The English were winning, but broke ranks when they thought William was dead. He wasn't; the Normans counter-attacked, during which Harold was shot above the eye with an arrow. He died and the English were overrun.

This was the famous Battle of Hastings. William then went on to take Dover and Canterbury.

He became William I of England on Christmas Day, 1066.

He soon returned to Normandy, leaving the Norman knights to tax and rob the English with brutal greed.

Norman versus Saxon hatred had the country close to revolt. There was a serious rebellion in the North; William wiped it out, and then razed the ground and buildings. For years, great stretches of territory became almost uninhabited. Many Saxons escaped to Scotland and sold themselves into slavery.

The last rebel was Hereward the Wake of Ely; however, he was eventually beaten.

By the end of the reign, ninety per cent of the land belonged to the Normans.

William had to overcome a revolt by the Norman barons, because they wanted even more than he was allowing them to take.

He caused the Domesday Book to be compiled to record everybody's value.

William I died in 1087 with two kingdoms.

William II 1087–1100

THIRTEEN YEARS

William I had three sons:

- Robert was to have the Duchy of Normandy;
- William Rufus (William II) was to have England;
- Henry was to have £5,000 in gold.

When Archbishop Lanfranc of Canterbury died, there was no reappointment and William II used the Church funds for himself.

When he was about to die, he repented and appointed Anselm as the Archbishop of Canterbury.

William recovered, regretted his decision, and after many arguments, drove Anselm into exile in Normandy.

William Rufus died by accident while hunting in the New Forest. An arrow from Sir Walter Tyrrell killed him.

His brother Henry was hunting with him at the time!

Henry I 1100–1135

THIRTY-FIVE YEARS

Henry became King of England, because his brother Robert was away on a crusade.

Henry took a Scottish wife called Matilda.

He then invaded Normandy, where his brother Robert was king. At the Battle of Tinchebrai, the English took revenge for Hastings.

Robert was taken prisoner for thirty years and died in Cardiff Castle.

Henry I now had England and Normandy. He also had one son named Prince William, who was drowned in the *White Ship* travelling from Normandy to England at the age of seventeen.

His daughter, Matilda, then became heir to the throne of England and Normandy.

Matilda 1141

Matilda was the daughter of King Henry I of England and Matilda of Scotland.

She was one of two children.

When her brother died at sea, she became the last heir from the paternal line of her grandfather, William the Conqueror.

As a child, Matilda was betrothed to Henry V, Holy Roman Emperor.

From this marriage, she acquired the title 'empress'. They had no known children.

When widowed, she was married to Geoffrey of Anjou (Plantagenet), by whom she had three sons, the eldest of whom became King Henry II of England.

Matilda was the first female ruler of England. However, the length of her effective rule was a mere few months in 1141.

She was never crowned, and failed to consolidate her rule either legally or politically.

Because of this, she is normally excluded from lists of English monarchs, and her rival and cousin Stephen of Blois is routinely listed as monarch for the period 1135–1154.

Their warring rivalry for the throne led to years of unrest and civil war in England that have been called the Anarchy.

She secured her inheritance of the Duchy of Normandy via the military feats of her husband Geoffrey.

She also campaigned unstintingly for her oldest son's inheritance and lived to see him ascend the throne of England as Henry II in 1154.

Along with Edward V, Edward VIII and Lady Jane Grey, Matilda is one of only four post-1066 monarchs never to have been crowned.

Stephen 1135–1154

NINETEEN YEARS

Henry I died and his daughter Matilda became queen. As Matilda was securing her position in Normandy, Stephen (Henry I's nephew) grabbed the English throne.

Matilda invaded from Normandy and beat Stephen. However, the English turned on Matilda and Stephen was released.

The battles of Stephen versus Matilda continued for five years, and then Matilda retired to Normandy. Her son Henry married the wealthy landowner Eleanor of Aquitaine.

Henry's next move was to invade England. Stephen's son died and so he made terms with Henry. This was known as the Peace of Wallingford.

In 1154 Henry became King of England.

Henry II 1154–1189

Henry II was the most powerful man in Europe.

- He acquired Aquitaine – from his wife.
- He acquired Normandy with Anjou – from his father.
- England was newly acquired.
- His power stretched from Spain to Scotland.
- Henry had a strong build – he was a great athlete and warrior.
- He spoke several languages.
- He also had a deep knowledge of the law (he was often called upon to settle disputes between foreign princes).

Henry made the barons pull down their illegal castles and sent away foreign mercenaries.

Thomas Becket became Chancellor, and was also a great friend of Henry. Later, he was made Archbishop of Canterbury, but he decided he couldn't serve two masters and so resigned the chancellorship. Continuous clashes occurred between Becket and Henry, which came to a climax over the matter of the Church and lay courts.

Many of the clergy or 'clerks' were receiving very light punishments for severe crimes because they were associated with the Church and were tried in the Church courts.

Henry wanted the clergy handed over to the lay courts. Becket refused to budge an inch. The quarrel became so bitter that Becket decided to flee abroad.

Six years later, because of papal pressure, Becket returned, but continued his clashes with Henry. Henry said in Normandy when in a fit of temper, that he despised his followers for not avenging him against this 'upstart clerk'. The knights responded to this taunt. They rode from Normandy and killed Becket inside Canterbury Cathedral. Henry was blamed for Becket's death and had to:

• Walk through the streets and be scourged by the monks.
• Make gifts to the church.
• Give up his plan to reduce the power of the church.

He then policed his dominions.

He cleared the northern counties of the Scots.

Warfare between the Irish chieftains and the involvement of Norman knights from South Wales made Henry invade and assert his authority in 1172.

Henry was accepted, and set up government in Dublin, but he didn't stay long to watch its progress.

Policing his vast dominions was a problem. The King of France only had a small area around Paris, and was discontented.

Queen Eleanor resided in Aquitaine with her sons, who became rebellious against Henry, since he gave them titles only, but no power.

Henry II's sons were:

• Henry
• Richard
• Geoffrey
• John.

In 1173, young Henry, Richard and Geoffrey joined

forces with King Louis of France against Henry II. The rebels were joined by the Scots and some English barons. Henry II was victorious everywhere and he pardoned his sons. His sons Henry and Geoffrey died a few years later, which meant that the conflict of power was now between Richard (Duke of Aquitaine) and the youngest son, John, who was Henry II's favourite.

In 1189 Richard sided with the French again and beat Henry II. When he heard that John had joined the rebels, Henry gave up and died in bitter despair.

Richard I became King of England.

Richard I 1189–1199

TEN YEARS

Richard was known as the Lionheart or Richard Coeur de Lion.

Just before Henry II died, Saladin, the Muslim leader, captured Jerusalem. Most of the lands won in the First Crusade in 1099 were lost.

The Pope called the leading monarchs of Europe to make a great crusade to regain the Holy City.

It included:

- Emperor Frederick Barbarossa of Germany;
- Philip Augustus of France;
- Henry II of England;
- Duke Leopold of Austria.

Henry II was too old, so he sent Richard.

Richard was:

- A thirty-three-year-old blond giant;
- Chivalrous;
- Fond of poetry and music;
- Passionate about battle;
- Often gallant and generous to opponents;
- Otherwise cruel and greedy like his brother;
- He was also homosexual.

Richard spent four months in England after his coronation raising money for the third crusade.

He raised money by selling offices of state and granting charters to towns.

For 10,000 marks he released William the Lion from doing homage.

During the crusade, England was left in the care of his mother, Eleanor, and the Chancellor, William Longchamp.

Richard travelled with Philip Augustus of France, paused to conquer Cyprus and to marry Princess Berengaria of Navarre.

When Richard arrived in Palestine, Philip Augustus had besieged Acre but with no success. Richard soon had success.

There were problems:

- Troops were dying from disease;
- The English and French were bickering;
- Philip Augustus was jealous of Richard I and returned to France;
- Duke Leopold of Austria quit;
- Richard was left with an army that was not well equipped.

He was forced to retreat, but he first made a treaty to preserve the 'pilgrims' route'.

In 1192, he heard that brother John was in collusion with Philip Augustus of France, so he set out for England.

He couldn't go through France. He was recognised in Vienna, captured by Leopold of Austria, and given to the German Emperor.

In 1194 Richard was freed after a large ransom was paid by the English people.

Once home, he pardoned John but within a few months he raised an army to cross the channel and recover his lost possessions from Philip Augustus.

He never returned. He was killed in 1199 in a minor skirmish when he himself was without armour.

Richard asked that John should succeed him.

Richard was a brave soldier, but not a good king. Of his ten years as king, only six months were spent in England.

John 1199–1216

SEVENTEEN YEARS

John was not the heir to the throne by birth. His older brother Geoffrey had a son called Arthur in Brittany. Arthur was only a boy.

Eleanor and the barons supported John.

At John's birth his father called him 'John Lackland' because the royal possessions had been divided among his brothers. Trying to find some for John caused most of the family quarrels.

He was doted on by his father but was despised by his brothers.

In the early days he tried to complete the Irish conquest but made a fool of himself.

Yet he showed a better understanding of ruling than did Richard.

Arthur tried to rise up in Aquitaine but he was routed and probably murdered by John.

Subsequently John lost Normandy. This was a blessing. England became England again. John delivered firm government but had a disastrous quarrel with the Church.

He ordered the monks at Canterbury to choose one of his friends as Archbishop, but they elected Stephen Langton.

John drove out the monks and seized the Church property.

He was excommunicated by the Pope. To this he responded by stealing the Church treasures and then hiring an army to attack William the Lion of Scotland.

He defeated the Scots, the Welsh and Irish chieftains.

The Pope then told Philip Augustus (Champion of the Church) to invade John's kingdom. John overcame this by making peace with Stephen Langton and surrendering England to the Pope.

John then unsuccessfully invaded France. He returned home to face rebellion.

John's greed and cruelty and giving of top posts to foreign ruffians destroyed the barons' loyalty.

In 1215 they rode to London to draw up a charter of their rights. In a field called Runnymede, John put his seal to the 'Great Charter' (Magna Carta). He promised to rule according to the laws and customs of the realm. Twenty-four barons were selected to ensure he did so.

John obtained a letter from the Pope freeing him of the Charter. He then ravaged the estates of those who had stood against him.

In despair, the barons invited Louis of France to be the King of England.

In 1216 Louis landed and there was civil war all that summer.

John was sick and broken spirited. He died of a fever in October 1216. His nine-year-old son became Henry III.

John was a bad son, a bad brother, a bad king and an unpleasant man.

Henry III 1216–1272

FIFTY-SIX YEARS

People began to rally around the new king. Louis was still strong in the South but was eventually driven out.

While Henry was a child, the country was ruled first by William Marshall, who died, and then by Hubert de Burgh.

At twenty years of age, Henry began to rule himself.

He had no ability to rule. He was weak and extravagant.

It was, however, a great period for religion and the arts. Many churches, cathedrals and colleges were built.

Hubert de Burgh was unfairly dismissed.

Again many of the chief posts were going to foreigners.

The barons protested and Henry heeded this.

He then married Eleanor of Provence, but gave the top jobs to her relations.

He allowed the Pope to impose heavy taxes and to fill the Church places with French and Italian priests.

The barons found a new leader in Simon de Montfort, Earl of Leicester.

Henry said he'd mend his ways, but then broke his word.

This caused 'the Barons' War', instigated by de Montfort.

They captured Henry and his son Edward.

De Montfort then summoned the Parliament of 1265. It included clergy, knights and commoners from each shire.

De Montfort is regarded as the founder and father of

the English Parliament, where the laws were for the first time written in English. Parliament means 'talking place'.

Prince Edward escaped, then beat and killed de Montfort at Evesham.

Edward took charge and Henry III had seven peaceful years before he died. Edward was returning from Palestine at the time.

Roger Bacon from Somerset was well known at this time. He became a monk and dedicated his life to scientific research. He was often hounded and accused of witchcraft.

Edward I 1272–1307

THIRTY-FIVE YEARS

Edward I was crowned:

- King of England
- Lord of Ireland
- Duke of Aquitaine.

He was called 'the Hammer of the Scots'.

Edward was thirty-three when he became king. He was a very tall man, who learned from his father's faults. He was also known as Edward Longshanks.

His first task was to subdue the Welsh. He invaded Wales in 1277 and defeated Llewellyn – the latter had to give back the lands won during the reign of Henry III. He was allowed to keep the title 'Prince' and return to North Wales. The Welsh rose again with Llewellyn as their leader. Edward put them down again and divided the principality into five shires. Llewellyn was killed. He then surrounded Snowdon (the rebels' refuge) with a ring of massive fortresses – one was Caernarfon Castle. This is where his son, Edward, was born and later made the Prince of Wales. This was the beginning of a new custom, and Wales was joined to England.

Edward I was a good soldier and a good ruler. He abolished many of the barons' private courts. He rooted out many dishonest sheriffs and judges. He encouraged the wool trade with Flanders. He kept the barons in a state of respect and obedience. He expelled the Jews from

England in 1290 when they ran out of money to support his wars against Scotland, Wales and Ireland.

In 1295, he introduced the Model Parliament.

In 1286, the Royal line of Scotland came to an end. Thirteen nobles put in a claim to the throne. The most notable were John Balliol and Robert Bruce. Both were descended from William the Lion's brother. Both had estates in England, for which they paid homage to Edward I.

Edward was invited to judge the claims so as to avoid civil war. He awarded the throne to John Balliol. The Scots felt Balliol was a puppet to Edward so they refused to serve against the French. At this, Edward invaded Scotland. He defeated the Scots at Dunbar, removed Balliol, and carried the coronation stone from Scone to Westminster. The problem seemed to be over, until a man called William Wallace killed an English soldier in a scuffle. He became outlawed, his wife was murdered and his home destroyed. Wallace's supporters grew in number and he had a good victory against the English at Stirling Bridge.

Edward I, who had been fighting in Flanders, returned to rout the Scots at Falkirk. Wallace escaped but was eventually betrayed. He was executed in London.

After this, twenty-five-year-old Robert Bruce (grandson of the claimant) returned to Scotland from England to meet Red Comyn, one of the Scottish leaders. They quarrelled and Bruce killed him with a dagger. Bruce fled to the hills and set himself up as the new champion.

He had no money and his followers were either executed or persecuted. His following eventually grew, despite this.

In 1307, Edward I set out to conquer Scotland for the third time. He was old and died as he reached the border.

Edward II 1307–1327

TWENTY YEARS

Edward I, as he was dying, made Edward II promise to defeat Robert Bruce. He disobeyed his father and turned south. He also recalled from exile his playfellow Piers Gaveston, to whom he gave many gifts and positions.

Eventually, some enraged nobles formed a committee (the Lords Ordainers) who took over government and banished Gaveston. Edward II recalled Gaveston and sent him to Scarborough Castle for safety. He was captured and executed.

Robert Bruce now had control of all Scotland except Stirling. If this went, English rule was finished.

Edward II finally stirred himself and took an army to Bannockburn. He was incompetent. The Battle of Bannockburn was the biggest English defeat since Hastings. Stirling was lost and English rule finished. Robert Bruce ruled Scotland.

Edward II was despised by all.

His new favourites were the Despensers (father and son). They too were unpopular. Edward then executed all his main opponents, overthrew the Ordainers and then took over government.

Queen Isabella and Prince Edward visited Paris, where Isabella fell in love with the exiled Roger Mortimer. Mortimer hated the Despensers.

In 1326 Isabella and Mortimer came to England to rid it of the Despensers. Edward II was deserted and captured. He was forced to give the crown to his son. He was then murdered in Berkeley Castle.

For three years, Isabella and Mortimer ruled in the name of young Edward III.

In 1330 Edward came to realise the greed of Mortimer and the disgraceful position of his mother.

He had Mortimer hanged at Tyburn like a criminal and his mother forced into isolated retirement.

Edward III 1327–1377

FIFTY YEARS

Edward III appeared at first to be the perfect monarch. He wanted battle honours.

He tried to recover Scotland when Bruce died and left his crown to his son David. Edward III put John Balliol's son on the throne and beat the Scots at Halidon Hill. The French helped the Scots by attacking Gascony (Edward's possessions in south-west France).

Edward III claimed the French crown via Isabella and prepared for war.

War began in 1340 with battles in Brittany and Gascony. This was the beginning of the 100 years war.

In 1346, the Battle of Crecy was fought. Edward III's son (the Black Prince) took part in this. The English were greatly outnumbered but had a notable victory. The Order of the Garter was created.

Calais was then besieged and won.

At this time, diseased black rats arrived via Weymouth to bring the 'Black Death' to England. It killed approximately a third of the population in both towns and villages. There were not enough people left to farm the land so food prices rose, despite parliamentary price pegging. So began the bad feeling between the lords and the peasants.

In 1355, the Black Prince again ravaged France. He became trapped with a small army at Poitiers. He tried to do a deal, but the French wanted revenge for Crecy. They were the favourites, and so began the Battle of Poitiers. The French were beaten; their king and prince were captured.

Edward III advanced to Paris. Both sides were exhausted and a truce was made in 1360.

Edward III gave up his claim to the French throne in return for Aquitaine, Gascony and Calais. The French king was released, but because his ransom could not be paid, he honourably returned to captivity in London, where he died.

Prince Edward (the Black Prince) went to live in Aquitaine. He became ill and returned to London, where he died in 1376. He would have made a good king.

During his absence, all except a few coastal towns in France returned to the French. Crecy and Poitiers were fully avenged.

In the latter part of Edward III's reign he faded. The king became old and feeble.

The Black Prince had died. The French possessions were lost. There was nothing to show for all the early glories.

The king began to lose his grip and discontentment became rife.

John Wycliffe and his wandering preachers found eager listeners when they attacked the clergy and nobles.

Edward III died in 1377. He had reigned for fifty years.

During his reign, John Wycliffe had also begun to teach and preach against the Pope having authority over the English Church. He also translated the Bible from Latin to English. His followers were called Lollards.

Geoffrey Chaucer (1340–1400), the great English writer, was born during this reign.

Richard II 1377–1399

TWENTY–TWO YEARS

Richard II was the son of the Black Prince.

He was only eleven years old when Edward III died. John of Gaunt was his uncle.

The 'Council of Nobles' governed for him. To pay for the French war, which had been so costly, they levied a poll tax, i.e. a tax on every poll or head in the realm. This hit the poor very hard and created a dangerous social climate.

Serfs and bondage still existed.

Wat Tyler from Kent killed a tax collector. An army of Kentish men formed behind him. They freed John Ball (the mad priest from Kent) from jail and marched to London to tell their grievances to the young king. They wanted the removal of the Council of Nobles.

From then on, the 'Peasants Revolt' grew in size. It became a lawless rabble.

They looted everywhere and murdered the Archbishop of Canterbury and the Lord Treasurer.

Richard met them at Smithfield and promised freedom from bondage if they went home quietly.

During the parley, Tyler leaned forwards towards his king. The Lord Mayor, William Walworth, feared for the young king's safety and stabbed Tyler to death.

When the danger passed, the nobles hunted down the ringleaders and hanged them. Richard II then promised the peasants even worse bondage.

Nevertheless, the old screws of feudalism were not

really tightened again. The peasants gained their freedom gradually. They eventually became landless labourers who worked for wages – poor, but not serfs.

Richard surrounded himself by elegant favourites and ruled badly. As a result a committee of nobles called the 'Lords Appellant' took over government and banished or executed the king's favourites.

At twenty-four years of age, Richard took power back again and for eight years ruled well.

- He made peace with France;
- He restored order in Ireland;
- He was tolerant of the Lollards.

Then his first wife died and he married the daughter of the King of France (Isabella). From this time his character changed. He had all his old opponents executed and their estates confiscated.

Richard then continued to behave almost insanely. He banished his cousin Henry Bolingbroke (John of Gaunt's son). When John of Gaunt died, Richard seized his estates and then sailed to Ireland.

In his absence, Henry Bolingbroke landed in England to claim back his father's land. His arrival sparked a rebellion – particularly by landowners who feared confiscation of their lands.

Richard returned and was made to sign over the throne to Henry Bolingbroke (Henry IV). He declared himself unfit to rule.

Richard was taken from the Tower to Pontefract Castle, where he was probably murdered in 1400.

Henry IV 1399–1413

FOURTEEN YEARS

Henry was a plain and sturdy man. He wasn't the real heir to the throne. The real heir was a child called Edward Mortimer.

As a usurper, Henry had to tread warily. He tried to subdue the Scots before they could assist the French, who would want revenge for Richard's death.

He was unable to bring the Scots to battle.

The Earl of Northumberland and his son, Henry Percy (Harry Hotspur), defeated the Scots and took many of their leaders.

Henry was faced with rebellion in Wales in the form of Owen Glendower, who felt he was wronged by Henry in the settling of a dispute with an English noble. When Henry marched on the Welsh they withdrew to the mountains. His second attempt was no more successful. Owen Glendower then captured Lord Grey and Sir Edmund Mortimer (uncle to the heir). He was master of Wales and lived as an independent monarch.

The Percies decided to join Glendower.

Mortimer became Glendower's son-in-law.

Henry saw the danger and tackled the Percies at the Battle of Shrewsbury.

Hotspur was slain and his father captured.

Glendower continued to defy the English king, but Prince Hal whittled away at him until he was ineffective. Prince Hal was the son of Henry IV and was therefore the Prince of Wales.

He succeeded to the throne as Henry V.

Henry V 1413–1422

NINE YEARS

As a prince, Henry V had practically ruled the country. He was one of the best-loved kings in history.

Henry decided to attack France:

- Because of their continual conspiring with Wales and Scotland;
- Because of the discontentment inside France;
- Because he convinced himself he had a right to the throne (he had *no* right).

Henry besieged and eventually won Harfleur. He then marched to Calais with 6,000 men. He was stopped at Agincourt by a large French army. Henry was hugely outnumbered.

The Battle of Agincourt was quickly and surprisingly won by Henry.

Half the nobility of France was killed or captured. The captured men were ransomed.

There followed the conquest of Normandy and the capture of Rouen.

Paris lay open to Henry but the French wanted peace.

It was agreed:

1. He should marry Catherine (the king's daughter);
2. He should rule France during the French king's lifetime;

3. After the French king's death, Henry and his heirs should succeed to the throne of France.

Henry visited England and then returned to France, where at thirty-three he died of dysentery.

Henry was at the height of his fame and popularity on both sides of the Channel.

Henry VI 1422–1461 and 1470–1471

FORTY YEARS

Henry became King of England when he was just a baby. After the death of Charles VI of France, he became the French king as well – according to the treaty.

As Regent of France, the Duke of Bedford had to control the French. He won several battles.

In 1428 he was about to take Orleans when Joan of Arc appeared. She was a country girl. She came to the court of the Dauphin, Charles, and said that God had spoken to her. She said that she would rid France of the English and that the Dauphin would be crowned in the church at Rheims.

She rode to Orleans, inspired the troops, relieved Orleans, and then beat the English at Patay.

Within a year Charles VII was crowned in Rheims Cathedral.

Joan of Arc wanted 'out' but stayed on by request. Joan made military mistakes. She failed at Paris and was captured by the Bergundians, who handed her over to the English. She was found guilty of witchcraft and was burned in the marketplace at Rouen.

The war continued to and fro, but the French gradually inched forwards until everything except Calais was again French. Even Aquitaine, which the English had had for 300 years since Henry II, was lost.

1453 marked the end of the Hundred Years War.

When Henry VI became an adult, he was timid and shrank from war. His attitudes were blamed for the English defeats in France.

His advisor, the Duke of Suffolk, was murdered.

The men of Kent rose up under Jack Cade.

They defeated the royal troops and started to loot London. They were then driven out by the citizens and Cade was killed. The rebellion fizzled out but it showed the disorder of the country.

The hostile parties were arming themselves.

1. Lancastrians – Red Rose – Royal supporters of Henry VI.
2. Yorkists – White Rose – Richard Duke of York's supporters.

Richard Duke of York was heir to the throne if Henry VI had no children.

In 1453 Henry became mad and Richard was made Protector of the Realm.

The childless Henry then had a son and heir to the throne. He recovered his wits and had Richard Duke of York dismissed. This then caused the War of the Roses – only two years after the end of the Hundred Years War. The two sides were as follows:

Lancastrians	**Yorkists**
Red Rose	*White Rose*
King Henry VI	Richard Duke of York
Queen Margaret	Earl of Salisbury
Duke of Somerset	Earl of Warwick
	Edward of March (York's eldest son)

There was a battle at St Albans in 1455, won by the

Yorkists.

The Duke of Somerset was killed and Henry went mad again.

Richard Duke of York took control of the kingdom, but Queen Margaret resisted. She raised an army which scattered the Duke's forces.

Queen Margaret then declared that the Yorkists forfeited their lives and estates. So, with nothing to lose, the Yorkists made another attack.

Warwick and Edward of March landed and had great support. Many people detested the queen. They defeated the royal army at Northampton in 1460.

Henry VI was captured and York claimed the crown. Henry agreed to this, which infuriated the queen, whose son was the rightful heir.

Queen Margaret raised another army. York did battle with her, lost and was killed. The Earl of Salisbury was executed and the queen then recovered the captive King Henry.

Then Warwick did battle with Margaret at St Albans again. Margaret won the battle and was in an overall winning position. But she made a mistake. Her troops were out of control and she didn't take London.

Warwick and Edward made a dash for London. At St Paul's, it was agreed that Henry was unfit to rule and that Edward March (York's son) should be king in his place. He became Edward IV.

Edward IV 1461–1470 and 1471–1483

TWENTY-ONE YEARS

Warwick and Edward IV then pursued the remainder of the Lancastrian army.

In 1461 the armies met at Towton in Yorkshire. The Lancastrians were routed, with the most terrible slaughter ever seen in battle in England.

Henry, his wife and son fled to Scotland. They later returned and Henry was taken prisoner and put in the Tower.

Warwick was all-powerful, since Edward IV was only interested in pleasure. He arranged for Edward to marry a French princess till Edward revealed that he was already wed to Elizabeth Woodville (the widow of a Lancastrian).

Edward became tired of being Warwick's puppet. He promoted all the Woodvilles and rid himself of Warwick's friends.

He forbade his brother Clarence to marry Warwick's daughter. Clarence disobeyed and did so. Clarence and Warwick then teamed up and Edward IV had to surrender.

Warwick now had two kings in his power:

1. Henry in the Tower
2. Edward IV in his camp.

Edward IV was so popular that he had to be released. He then drove Warwick out to France. Edward IV's opponents now were:

* Earl of Warwick
* Queen Margaret and son
* Clarence (his brother).

All were seeking refuge in France.

King Louis of France suggested that Warwick should now remove Edward IV from the throne and replace him with the imprisoned Henry VI.

Margaret and her supporters agreed to this. When they landed in England, Edward fled to Flanders without a fight.

Warwick, 'the Kingmaker', took Henry out of the Tower in 1470 and put him on the throne.

Clarence didn't like having the Lancastrians back on the throne. He agreed to desert Warwick when the time was right and join Edward.

Then Edward landed, gathered an army and marched on Warwick. Clarence duly deserted Warwick and joined Edward. Warwick was defeated and killed.

On the same day, Margaret and her son Edward landed and were defeated at Tewkesbury. The son was killed and Margaret was sent to the Tower, where old Henry was murdered. Clarence was imprisoned for the rest of his life.

Edward IV now had no opponents for the rest of his reign.

He invaded France in order to punish King Louis for his interference but accepted a large sum of money not to do battle.

Edward V 1483

Edward IV died leaving two small sons.

The elder one became King Edward V from 9 April 1483 for a period of two months, but was not crowned.

He was only thirteen years old when his father died.

It was decided that Edward IV's brother, Richard of Gloucester, should be made protector until the boy was older.

The two princes were placed in the Tower for 'safety'. They disappeared.

Along with Edward VIII, Empress Matilda and Lady Jane Grey, Edward V is one of only four post-1066 monarchs never to have been crowned. If, as seems probable, he died before his fifteenth birthday, he is the shortest-lived monarch in English history.

Richard III 1483–1485

TWO YEARS

Richard removed all opposition, then claimed the throne since he said Edward IV's marriage was illegal. He was then crowned Richard III.

Edward V and his brother were presumed murdered in the Tower on Richard's instructions. They were never seen again. Twenty years later, Sir James Tyrell confessed to killing them.

Richard III was called 'Crookback'. He was a first-class general and very brave.

All opposition was removed except for one man. He was the last hope of the Lancastrians – Henry Tudor, Earl of Richmond.

He had been sent to Brittany for his safety.

Henry was the descendant of Edward III. His grandfather was Owen Tudor.

He landed at Milford Haven and collected support. Henry was hoping that some of Richard III's supporters would fade away and that Lord Stanley and Sir William Stanley would assist him.

Richard III and Henry met to do battle at Bosworth Field in Leicestershire (1485).

At a critical time, the Stanley brothers changed sides. Richard was killed and Henry became Henry VII – first of the Tudor monarchs.

Henry VII 1485–1509

TWENTY-FOUR YEARS

Henry was the first of the Tudor monarchs.

He was no warrior. He would fight if it was necessary but not by choice.

Henry was very interested in the business of the kingdom. He set out to restore the force of law and to settle the Yorkist–Lancastrian feud.

He married Elizabeth of York, the sister of the two princes who disappeared from the Tower.

He ordered the barons to dismiss their private armies. Those who disobeyed were heavily fined.

For fifteen years Henry overcame his difficulties by skill and cunning.

A baker's son named Lambert Simnel claimed to be Edward Plantagenet. He was crowned in Ireland. Henry routed the boy's supporters and put Simnel to work in the royal kitchen.

Then the Yorkists produced Perkin Warbeck. He claimed to be Richard of York – the younger of the two princes in the Tower. He claimed that he escaped when his older brother was murdered.

From Ireland, Warbeck went to Flanders, where Margaret of York 'recognised' him as her nephew. Henry threatened to stop the Flemish wool trade. Warbeck then went to Scotland, where he married into the Scottish nobility.

Henry then found that his old friend, Sir William Stanley, was playing a double game. Henry had him arrested and executed.

Meanwhile a rising of discontented Cornishmen persuaded Warbeck to try his luck in the West Country. Henry marched on them. The rebellion fizzled out. A few were hanged and some were fined. Warbeck was treated with mercy but later his own folly caused him to be hanged in the Tower.

After this Henry's troubles became fewer. Most of his rivals had been killed off. The throne was safe. Henry decided that to increase his power he must increase his wealth.

He punished offenders by fines.

He encouraged 'gifts' and taxes from his subjects.

He even invaded France and then accepted a vast pay-off to return home without fighting.

Under this wily king, the country prospered. Henry arranged for his eldest son, Arthur, to marry Catherine of Aragon – daughter of the King of Spain.

His daughter, Margaret, married James IV of Scotland.

Christopher Columbus made his immortal voyage of 1492 during his reign. The English sea captains were not interested in such discoveries.

There was in Bristol another Genoese – John Cabot. He wanted to find the Spice Islands in the East by sailing west. Henry sponsored him because he knew the other monarchs of Europe were doing similar sponsorships. Cabot set sail in the *Matthew* in 1497. He discovered Newfoundland. He was disappointed in this.

He tried again to find the spice lands. He got to America and sailed south hoping to find a channel. Again he failed and returned to Bristol a puzzled man.

Henry VII became a sad figure at the end of his reign. He was ill himself. Also there were the deaths of his wife and eldest son Arthur. His popularity had gone and his ministers were hated for their greed.

He left a vigorous, wealthy, well-run kingdom.

Caxton brought the art of printing to England during this reign.

Henry VIII 1509–1547

THIRTY-EIGHT YEARS

- Henry VIII became king at eighteen.
- He was 6' 2" and a good athlete who spoke five languages.
- Henry also wrote poetry and played musical instruments. He also composed music.
- He was good at all sport and he was handsome.
- Henry was a great spender.
- He executed his father's unpopular ministers.
- He married Catherine of Aragon – the widow of his brother, Arthur.

Thomas Wolsey had been secretary to the Archbishop of Canterbury and then to Henry VIII. He was young and talented. Henry VIII picked him out to manage the kingdom.

Henry wanted to do battle with France. Wolsey organised this. The French were routed at the Battle of the Spurs. Although not a great battle, Henry was satisfied that Europe had seen an English king in action again.

During Henry's absence, James IV of Scotland had attacked England. Queen Catherine sent the Earl of Surrey to the Borders, where in 1513 he won the Battle of Flodden. This was the last great victory won by the longbow. James IV was killed during the battle. Scotland was then ruled by the widowed Queen Margaret who was the daughter of Henry VII and the sister of Henry VIII.

In France, Henry VIII and Wolsey made peace and sent

Henry's beautiful sister to marry the old French king, who soon died and was succeeded by the young and masterful Francis I.

Henry VIII and Francis I were well matched. Wolsey continued to manage the kingdom and grew richer as he did so. He had many high positions in the Church and owned lots of land. The Pope made him a Cardinal. He not only managed the kingdom but ruled the Church also. All this would continue as long as he pleased Henry.

After eighteen years of marriage Henry had only one daughter by Catherine. Her name was Mary. Five other children had died in babyhood. He badly wanted a son and heir. He decided he had no son because he had sinned in marrying his brother's wife. He wanted a divorce so that he could marry Anne Boleyn and have a son. It was for Wolsey to arrange this with the Pope. This should have been a mere formality but the Pope was in a difficult position. Rome was occupied by Charles V, who was Catherine's nephew. A divorce would offend Charles and this he could not do. The matter was delayed for months and Wolsey could not get the answer Henry wanted.

Henry blamed Wolsey for all this. He stripped him of most of his wealth and banished him from court. Wolsey retired to York. He was then charged with treason and died at Leicester while on his way back to London.

Henry then appointed Sir Thomas More as Chancellor. He defied the Pope by putting Catherine aside. Archbishop Cranmer announced his marriage to Anne Boleyn. Parliament declared the marriage legal and made Henry 'Supreme Head on earth, under God, of the Church of England'. The leading men of the kingdom were made to swear an oath to accept this state of affairs. Sir Thomas More, who had already resigned the Chancellorship, refused to do so. The Duke of Norfolk urged him to do so. The case against Thomas More was instigated by Thomas Cromwell. More was eventually executed. Cromwell then became Chancellor and was as grasping as Wolsey. Henry and Cromwell carried out the Reformation, in which they closed the monasteries, seized their wealth and sold their lands. The Protestants grew in numbers. Many people didn't want to see the authority of the Pope restored, since they would have to give lands back to the Church.

Henry changed from jovial monarch to suspicious despot. He had more real power than any ruler of England before or since.

He was as ruthless in his private life as in his public life.

With Anne Boleyn he had Elizabeth. Two sons were born dead. Anne was executed on a trumped up charge of infidelity.

He then married Jayne Seymour, who died giving birth to Edward.

He then married Anne of Cleves, a German princess. Thomas Cromwell arranged this. Ann turned out to be ugly. She was set aside and Cromwell was beheaded for his failure.

Henry then married Catherine Howard. She was lovely and sinful – and executed.

Henry was now generally hated and feared.

He defied the Pope and two great monarchs abroad. He subdued Wales and Ireland and thrashed the Scots at Solway Moss. The Scottish king died leaving a daughter – Mary Queen of Scots.

Henry's last wife was mainly a companion for his old age; her name was Catherine Parr.

Near the end of his reign Henry invaded France and had some small success. The French tried to invade England but it came to nothing.

Henry became plagued by an ulcer to the leg which was killing him.

Because Edward was too young to rule, Henry chose a

council of ministers to look after the country if he were to die. It included men of the old and new faiths.

Henry died after thirty-eight years as king.

He had had six wives:

1. Catherine of Aragon (who gave birth to Mary);
2. Anne Boleyn (Elizabeth);
3. Jane Seymour (Edward);
4. Anne of Cleves;
5. Catherine Howard;
6. Catherine Parr.

Their fates can be remembered by the rhyme:
Divorced, beheaded, died – divorced, beheaded, survived.

Edward VI 1547–1553

SIX YEARS

Shortly after Henry's death the council began to disobey his orders. A party of extreme Protestants took charge.

Their leader was Jane Seymour's brother. He made himself Protector and Duke of Somerset.

They attacked the Roman Catholic religion and seized the rest of the Church properties. Riots and risings broke out. Soon the country was in a state of chaos and disorder.

Somerset was overthrown and executed by John Dudley (Duke of Northumberland). He became master of the kingdom and of Edward.

Chaos continued. Rents and prices rose and the value of wages fell. England was almost bankrupt.

Northumberland merely increased his own power. He completely controlled the pro-Protestant Edward until he was fifteen years old. At this age he had measles which led to lung disease. He was clearly going to die.

The heirs to the throne were:

1st   Mary
2nd   Elizabeth
3rd   Frances, Duchess of Suffolk.

The Duchess of Suffolk was Henry's niece. She had a daughter – Lady Jane Grey.

Northumberland persuaded the Duchess to pass her claim to Jane Grey. He then arranged for Jane to marry his son, Guildford Dudley. Jane had no choice.

Northumberland pressured the dying king to leave his kingdom to Lady Jane Grey. The Privy Council was bullied into accepting this illegal scheme. Edward died and Jane was proclaimed Queen of England by Northumberland. Jane was not happy with this charade, which lasted just nine days.

Mary I 1553–1558

FIVE YEARS

Northumberland wanted to seize Princess Mary, who had ridden to Framlingham Castle in Suffolk. The English resented Northumberland's scheme to cheat Mary of the crown, even though she was a Catholic. Research shows that Edward VI gave heavy support to this scheme, since he was so fanatically Protestant and because Mary was a Catholic.

Northumberland was defeated by Mary's supporters. He was taken to the Tower and executed. He shamefully renounced the Protestant faith for which he had committed his crimes.

Mary tried to convert the imprisoned Lady Jane Grey to change her faith. Because of her refusal Mary had to order the execution of her cousin for treason. Alive, Jane would always be the cause of plots and rebellion, even though she did not really want the crown. Jane was only sixteen when executed.

Mary put her half-sister Elizabeth in prison and then under house arrest at Hatfield near St Albans. She stayed there till Mary died.

Mary was nearing middle age when she came to the throne. Years of sorrow and humiliation gave her a severe expression. She was brave and kinder than the rest of the Tudors. The people liked her mother, and admired the way Mary had stood up to Northumberland.

Mary made the mistake of wanting to bring England back to the Pope's authority with all speed. Catholic bishops were released from prison. Leading Protestants were removed from office. There was no effort to return the Church lands. Services were held as they were in Henry VIII's last years.

Mary's fatal mistake was to marry her cousin, Philip of Spain. This was unpopular. The English didn't want to be part of the great Spanish Empire.

The arrival of Cardinal Pole from Rome inflamed things even more. Mary was not dismayed by the opposition, and pressed on to teach her subjects obedience.

Persecution of the Protestants began in 1555 with the burning of Bishop Hooper and John Rogers at Smithfield.

By the end of the year seventy people had died. They included Bishops Latimer and Ridley.

Cranmer, now old, confessed the errors of his ways and agreed that he was responsible for all the ills the Church had endured. At the end, he regained his courage and went to the stake a Protestant, thrusting first into the flames the hand which signed the confession.

Altogether about 300 Protestants were burned alive. This was not many by continental standards, but it earned great hate for the Catholic Church.

Mary's life was a tragedy for the following reasons:

- Philip left her to look after Spain;
- She had no children;
- Her religion became hated;
- She lost Calais (our last foreign possession) to the French;
- Seriously ill and crushed by unhappiness, she died after only five years as queen.

Elizabeth I 1558–1603

FORTY-FIVE YEARS

Elizabeth was Henry VIII's second daughter.

She had been closely guarded during the previous two reigns. Her sharp wit had often saved her. She was twenty-five, red-haired and handsome.

Elizabeth was neglected by her father, but was still well educated and loved sport and music. She had a great presence and a dominant personality.

Elizabeth also had Henry VIII's temper, some of his meanness but none of his cruelty.

For forty-five years she inspired love and obedience from her people. She never really trusted anyone.

Her chances of survival were slim. In her kingdom, and abroad, there was bitter enmity between the Protestants and the Catholics.

Philip of Spain was interested in adding England to his empire. He offered to marry Elizabeth. She didn't want him because of the religious problem, but didn't want to pay the price of offending him. She played him along.

At this time, France was more dangerous than Spain.

The King of France (Henry II) had captured Calais and wanted more success. He had a good hold on Scotland, where Mary Queen of Scots' mother, a French princess, was ruling Scotland, with the help of French troops.

Henry II arranged for his son to marry Mary Queen of Scots who, in Catholic eyes, was the rightful Queen of England. Elizabeth and Mary were cousins. It was a worry that Henry might aspire to wanting England and Scotland as part of his empire. It was a dangerous situation.

Elizabeth played her cards cleverly.

- She solved the religious problem by tolerance. She neither favoured nor persecuted any religion as long as it didn't upset the state. She neither pleased nor displeased any religion. In the first eleven years of her reign, not one person was burnt for religion or executed for treason.
- She played Philip along, and thereby knew he would not tolerate his great enemy, the King of France, putting Mary Queen of Scots onto the English throne.
- In Scotland she was lucky. John Knox, a fiery Protestant, had returned from exile. He preached hatred of the Catholic religion. As a result, the Scots drove out the occupying French forces. Scotland was then free of French influence. Subsequently, incidentally Henry sent more troops to Scotland, but his fleet was destroyed by a gale at sea.

Henry II of France died from a tournament injury. His son became Francis II, and Mary Queen of Scots was Queen of France as well as having a claim to the English throne.

It looked dangerous, but Francis II died suddenly, and Mary Queen of Scots was not welcome in France. She returned to Scotland.

She was nineteen and beautiful. She tried to win the hearts of the people and also to come to terms with Knox.

Mary then made the mistake of marrying her cousin, Lord Darnley. Darnley proved to be an arrogant waster. Mary soon despised him and gave him no part in ruling the kingdom. He then plotted against Mary.

In a fit of rage, Darnley and some ruffians broke into the queen's room, dragged out her Italian secretary, David Rizzio, and murdered him.

Not long afterwards, Darnley was also found dead in Edinburgh. It is not known if Mary had any part in this.

The Earl of Bothwell was charged with the crime but then acquitted, thanks to the presence of his own troops in the city.

Three months later, Mary Queen of Scots married Bothwell. The Scots regarded Bothwell as a murderer and were disgusted by Mary's conduct. They drove Mary from the throne in favour of her infant son, James. She was imprisoned in a castle on an island in Loch Leven and she was separated from her child.

Mary escaped, raised an army and did battle with Moray, the Scottish Regent. She lost but escaped. She was unable to get a boat to France so she made for England, where she asked Elizabeth for help.

This posed a problem for Elizabeth...

- If she helped Mary regain her throne, she offended the Protestants.
- If she handed Mary back to her captors, it would infuriate the Catholics.
- If she let Mary go abroad, she would get armed help to satisfy her ambitions.

Faced with these dilemmas, Elizabeth chose to do nothing. She kept Mary half guest and half prisoner in various northern castles for the next nineteen years. Elizabeth actually refused to see her in public.

Mary tried throughout to escape and recover the throne. She never lost courage and was always writing to friends for help. Elizabeth's spies fed her with all this information, including some of Mary's secret letters. Sir Francis Walsingham was her spy master who collected this information.

During this period, the Duke of Norfolk, cousin to Elizabeth and one of her favourites, was executed for plotting to put Mary on the English throne.

Elizabeth didn't want to execute Mary but when treason

was proved and Mary would not publicly beg forgiveness, her execution was inevitable.

Wearing red, and showing great courage, she was beheaded in Fotheringay Castle.

Those who had made Mary abdicate brought her son James up safely in Scotland.

Meanwhile Elizabeth held the stage like a great actress.

She played the following roles:

* Imperial monarch
* Scholarly queen
* Huntress
* Lovesick maiden
* Boisterous hoyden

She loved flattery but her head *always* ruled her heart – even with her favourite, the Earl of Leicester. This was the difference between Elizabeth and Mary Queen of Scots.

Elizabeth's faithful minister was Mr Secretary Cecil. Against mounting opinion, Elizabeth would not marry to produce a Protestant heir. She knew that almost any husband would bring disaster to England.

* An English or Scottish lord would arouse jealousy.
* A Protestant would incite Catholic rebellion.
* A Catholic would infuriate the Protestants.
* A Frenchman would cause war with Spain.

She remained unmarried although she was always sweet on the Earl of Leicester (previously Lord Robert Dudley). She was most upset when he married someone else.

Meanwhile, most of the wealth at sea belonged to Spain and Portugal who had divided the New World between them.

William Hawkins from Plymouth became a part-time pirate against the Spanish and Portuguese ships carrying gold and silver. Hawkins built a private fleet, which he would loyally use for the queen's service. She knew this, but when Philip of Spain protested, she denied all knowledge of these things.

William's son, John Hawkins, continued the family business, and extended it to slave trading between West Africa and Spanish America.

John Hawkins and Francis Drake were cousins. An incident involving these two against the Spanish in the port of San Juan marked the beginning of an undeclared war between the English and Spanish seamen.

The Spanish called Drake the 'Master Thief'.

In the *Golden Hind* he circumnavigated the world. The queen knighted him on his ship when he returned. The pirate trade in the Caribbean grew.

Other adventurers of this time included:

- Sir Richard Grenville
- Sir Humphrey Gilbert
- Sir Walter Raleigh
- Martin Frobisher.

Philip of Spain still wanted to restore the Catholic religion in the Netherlands and England. He sent the Duke of Parma to subdue the Dutch, who then appealed for help. Elizabeth sent a small army under the command of Leicester. Leicester's nephew, Sir Philip Sidney, also went and distinguished himself. He was eventually killed.

The execution of Mary Queen of Scots triggered Philip's desire to invade England and overthrow Elizabeth.

Mary had left her claim, not to her son James, but to Philip of Spain.

William Cecil became Lord Burghley.

Philip built a large fleet known as the Armada to carry stores and men to the Duke of Parma, who would be responsible for the invasion of England.

England prepared herself. Drake sailed into Cadiz harbour and destroyed thirty-seven warships.

In 1588, the great Armada set sail. Of the 130 ships, fifty were warships.

The English fleet was at Plymouth under Lord Howard. Drake, Hawkins and Frobisher each had a squadron.

Because of poor wind conditions, a confused battle took place, lasting for a week. The English were running out of ammunition but could not break up the Spanish formation. Then the wind got up and Howard used fireships at night to confuse and disperse the Armada. The English continued to attack and only fifty-three ships returned beaten to Spain.

Drake's later attack on Corunna failed.

During the course of time, Grenville, Frobisher, Drake and Hawkins all died at sea doing battle with the Spanish.

Eight years after the Armada, Philip's fleet at Cadiz was beaten by Howard, Raleigh and Essex. This marked the end of a long struggle.

Raleigh introduced tobacco and potatoes to England.

The population of England grew and unemployment became a feature. Poverty was rife, hence Elizabeth's Poor Laws. This made it the duty of every parish to look after its poor.

The Commons wanted more say in government. Social difficulties grew at the end of Elizabeth's reign, although there was mounting prosperity.

The greatest genius of the Elizabethan age was the son of a Warwickshire corn merchant and glove maker. He was William Shakespeare of Stratford-upon-Avon, who married Ann Hathaway.

At the end of her reign, Elizabeth had Essex executed for rebellion, despite their quite intimate relationship, and the fact that he was the son of her adored Leicester (who had died by this time).

She died, tired and lonely, on 24 March 1603.

She named James VI of Scotland to succeed her.

James I 1603–1625

James was both King of Scotland and of England. He was the only son of Mary, Queen of Scots and Darnley. After he was taken away from his mother he was brought up as a Protestant.

He was delicate, unable to stand easily, and had to be strapped to the saddle when hunting. As a child he was timid, intelligent and lonely. He was a puppet in the hands of his violent Scottish nobles, but when he grew up he managed to subdue them by trickery.

He ruled Scotland well and caused no offence to his cousin, Elizabeth I, even when his mother was sentenced to death.

He dressed badly, seldom washed, was lame and spoke oddly.

When he became King of England he showed great favouritism to Scottish courtiers and was pro-Church of England. He allowed the persecution of other religions, including the Catholics. As a result of this there was the Gunpowder Plot.

The conspirators wanted to kill the king and the leading men of the country when they assembled for the opening of Parliament.

The conspirators included Robert Catesby, Thomas Percy and a Yorkshireman named Guy Fawkes. Guy Fawkes was an explosives expert.

They hired a large storeroom right underneath the House of Lords, and into this managed to take thirty-six barrels of gunpowder. These were concealed under coals and firewood.

One of the conspirators warned his kinsman, Lord Monteagle, by letter that he should retire to the country to avoid a terrible blow. This letter was passed to the Council on 4 November 1605. As a result, an inspection of the cellars was made.

Fawkes was arrested and admitted to wanting to blow the Scots back to Scotland. He was tortured but refused to name the plotters. He was so maimed that he had to be carried to the gallows.

The Gunpowder Plot ruined the Catholic cause in England.

James I fell out with Parliament as a result of his belief in the Divine Right of Kings. He considered that all rights and privileges to people were gifts from the king, which could be withdrawn.

Parliament protested and was dismissed. James ruled for ten years without Parliament.

During his reign, Raleigh was charged with treason and sent to the Tower for the next thirteen years. James I was short of money and released Raleigh to fetch gold from El Dorado in 1616. The mission was a complete failure. Two years later, James sentenced Raleigh to death by execution.

In 1620, a band of Puritans set out from Plymouth in the *Mayflower* for Virginia.

They missed Virginia and arrived at New England. The settlement was called New Plymouth.

The leaders of the Pilgrim Fathers were William Bradford, John Carver and Miles Standish.

Life was hard but they survived and flourished.

James I died in 1625 leaving the kingdom much weaker than when he came to the throne twenty-two years before.

This failure was caused by a shortage of money, Parliament's demands to have a bigger say in government, the rising influence of the Puritans, and the feeling that the Church of England was becoming too much like the Church of Rome.

The decline was accelerated by James's lack of dignity, tact and charm.

One of his few successes was his authorisation in 1611 of the printing of a translation of the Bible.

This book is still known as the King James Bible, and demonstrates the beauty of the English language.

Charles I 1625–1649

TWENTY-FOUR YEARS

Charles was handsome, had a noble air of dignity and an appreciation of fine things. He also believed in the Divine Right of Kings.

Charles lacked the power to make sharp decisions and had a genius for taking bad advice. His double-dealing made it impossible for anybody to trust him.

The Duke of Buckingham, a close friend of Charles, arranged for him to marry Henrietta Maria, the King of France's sister, who was a Catholic. This annoyed the mainly Protestant Parliament.

Henrietta Maria grew to be an obstinate woman, devoted to her husband, forever inciting him to ignore Parliament and rule as he pleased.

The war with Spain was disastrous. A naval attack on Cadiz was a complete fiasco. Many of the ships had not been refitted since the Armada. This was another failure from Buckingham.

Buckingham then decided to make war on France and was defeated at La Rochelle. He was preparing further disasters when assassinated at Portsmouth.

Charles was now on terrible terms with Parliament and three times dismissed them. To obtain money, he made forced loans from every county and imprisoned those who refused to pay.

Parts of the country were under military law. In 1628, because of his lack of money he decided to call Parliament and to accept 'the Petition of Right'.

Because of his belief in the Divine Right, Charles again dismissed Parliament, and for another eleven years he ruled without one.

'Ship money', a wartime tax levied in counties near the sea, was then demanded from all counties. This caused indignation, since it had not been passed by Parliament.

Charles's chief ministers were Thomas Wentworth, who became Earl of Strafford, and William Laud, the Archbishop of Canterbury.

Wentworth led a strong government and managed with great efficiency. He was then sent to rule Ireland by the same stern system and brought the country to a state of order it had not known for centuries.

Wentworth was successful and was known by the king's opponents as 'Black Tom Tyrant'.

Strafford was feared, but Archbishop Laud was hated. He tried to reform the Church of England. He inspected parishes, punished the clergy for errors and tried to crush Puritanism. Charles and Laud then tried to do the same to Scotland. This was violently rejected since their methods too much resembled Popery.

Charles withdrew, and then sent for Strafford to come from Ireland to put the Scots in their place. The Scots were too much for him.

In the Bishops' War, the Scots captured Newcastle and refused to go home until paid to do so. Charles, with no money, had to summon Parliament.

'The Long Parliament' was called in 1640 and lasted for many years. It was led by John Hampden and John Pym. They were determined that the king would rule according to custom and law, and they were determined to put an end to Strafford. They tried to accuse Strafford of treason but were unable to do so. They therefore passed a Bill of Attainder. This declared him to be worthy of death but required the king's consent. Pym arranged rioting and eventually the king's nerve broke and he signed the death warrant.

After this, things grew worse. The Royalist party, known as the Cavaliers, began to arm. On the other hand, the Puritans were becoming very strong.

Charles tried to arrest Pym and Hampden, but failed.

The king moved to York to raise an army. Parliament and the Puritans also prepared for war.

Pym engaged Philip Skippon to drill the citizen forces.

In the country, Hampden and Oliver Cromwell began to train their tenants and Puritan yeomen. They became known as the Roundheads. The first battle of the Civil War was fought at Edgehill in 1642.

Parliament's general was the Puritan Earl of Essex.

The king's general was Prince Rupert, his nephew.

There was no outright victory or defeat on either side. Charles should have taken London but instead moved to Oxford, where he set up his headquarters. By the time the Royalists advanced on London, there was organised opposition, despite there being a much higher quality of Royalist cavalry.

For the next two years Charles seemed certain to win.

The Royalist cavalry under Rupert continued to outclass the opposition. When Rupert and his brother captured Bristol, Parliament's defeat seemed certain. At this time, Cromwell returned to East Anglia to train a force of Puritans who would fight, not for plunder, but for religion and for liberty.

Pym sent to the Scots for help and the Royalist victories were checked. The king could not take control and lacked a man of Strafford's strong ability. His friend Digby gave him bad advice, and Rupert was too hot-headed.

In two great battles, the war was lost.

At Marston Moor in 1644, the Scots, and Cromwell's new cavalry were too much for Rupert.

At Naseby, a year later, Fairfax and Cromwell destroyed the king's infantry.

Eventually Charles gave himself up to a Scottish army in Nottinghamshire. He preferred to surrender to the Scots, rather than Parliament's men.

The Scots wanted their Presbyterian religion to be made the official religion of England, and when Charles refused they handed him over to Parliament. Pym and Hampden were already dead, but Parliament had won.

The king was a prisoner in Holdenby House in Northamptonshire. All they needed was to make sure he ruled properly, when the army was sent home. The army would not disband in case their efforts had been in vain. Cromwell brought the king to army headquarters and he was soon lodged comfortably at Hampton Court. He was amused that Parliament, the army and the Scots were all at loggerheads. He refused the army's generous terms, by which he could have regained the throne. He then escaped to the Isle of White, where he took refuge at Carisbrooke Castle.

Charles then promised the Scots he would establish their religion in England if they would rescue him and overthrow the English army. Cromwell was furious and defeated the Scots. He dealt with Parliament by sending to Westminster, Colonel Pride, who turned anyone away who did not support Cromwell and the army leaders.

After Pride's Purge, about fifty members of the Long Parliament were left and this was nicknamed 'the Rump Parliament'.

The king was put on trial for high treason.

On 13 January 1649,[1] Charles was executed. This was an unpopular decision with the people of England.

---

1   Some sources give the date of execution as 20 January 1649.

The Protectorate:
Oliver Cromwell 1649–1658 and Richard Cromwell 1658–1659

TEN YEARS

After the execution, it was decided there would be no more kings. The House of Lords was abolished.

Many people were outraged at the king's death. The Scots and the Irish were particularly angry, and in Ireland a rebellion broke out against the English.

Cromwell took a New Model Army to Dublin. Being Puritans, they detested the Catholics and had not forgotten the massacre of Protestants during the previous Irish rebellion.

Cromwell subdued the country by killing priests, killing prisoners, and transporting thousands overseas. He confiscated Catholic estates. Cromwell's name is still a curse in Ireland.

Cromwell then turned his attention to the Scots, who had proclaimed Charles II as king. He won a crushing victory at Dunbar but Charles escaped.

Charles raised an army in England but at Worcester he was beaten by Cromwell. He again escaped and disguised himself as a labourer. Charles was continually on the run; he even hid in an oak tree at Boscobel House. Although he had considerable support, most people were frightened of Cromwell's 'Ironsides'.

After the battle of Worcester, it took Charles six

weeks to escape by boat to Normandy. Cromwell in the meantime became all powerful.

Cromwell found two fine soldiers/admirals in Robert Blake and General Monk. These two between them checked the growing Dutch sea power, which was thwarting English trading.

Because of poor and inefficient government, the Rump Parliament was dismissed by Cromwell. He did not dare allow free elections since he feared a return of a Royalist parliament. As a result, Cromwell ruled as Lord Protector of England, Scotland, Wales, Ireland and The Commonwealth, together with his New Model Army and his fine fleet.

England again became highly respected upon the continent and very prosperous. In his dictatorial attempts to give good government, Cromwell became more of a tyrant than Charles I had ever been. When opposition grew, he divided the country into districts under military law. The people hated Cromwell's puritanical rule but feared him too much to overthrow him. He ruled the country almost single-handed for nine years before he died at Whitehall in 1658.

He was succeeded by his son, Richard Cromwell (Tumble-down Dick). Richard had no wish to be a dictator; he resigned and went into the country.

In 1660, Charles II took the throne amidst scenes of joy never known before or since.

Charles II 1660–1685

TWENTY-FIVE YEARS

Years of travel had hardened Charles. He was charming, clever and interested in sport, science and architecture. He seemed to have no aim but to enjoy life.

He was determined to rule as he pleased at all costs. His new 'Cavalier Parliament' was filled by the king's friends, and although he persecuted those who had executed Charles I, there was a general pardon for the rest.

Charles seemed to lack gratitude for those Royalists who had lost so much for his father's cause.

There were harsh laws against those who did not conform to the Church of England, even though Charles was secretly a Roman Catholic.

Among the non-conformists or dissenters was John Bunyan, who wrote *Pilgrim's Progress* from Bedford Jail.

Early in Charles II's reign, war broke out against the Dutch. The king's brother, James, Duke of York, Prince Rupert and General Monk were capable generals and contained the enemy. But the navy was badly mismanaged. Dishonesty in the shipyards meant that the ships were badly equipped. The Navy therefore began to suffer defeats.

The plague was a regular visitor to London, but in 1665, the outbreak of the plague in London was severe. Thousands upon thousands died, and many began to flee to the country. Samuel Pepys chronicled events in his diary at this time.

So many people died that there were mass burials in

great pits. Filthy streets and rat-infested buildings helped to spread the plague.

When winter arrived the plague slowly died away, but the next year in September 1666, after a long spell of dry weather, a fire broke out in a baker's shop in Pudding Lane, near London Bridge.

The wind fanned the fire, and an area from the Tower to the Temple was soon blazing. Eventually, gunpowder was used to blow up whole blocks of houses to control the fire. In four days, over 13,000 houses, churches and public buildings were destroyed. This was the Great Fire.

London was rebuilt in brick and stone instead of timber and became the most handsome capital city in Europe.

Sir Christopher Wren devoted his genius to rebuilding the churches and also the building of St Paul's Cathedral.

After this, Britain, Holland and Sweden formed an alliance to protect themselves against Louis of France.

Charles, however, made a secret treaty with Louis, promising help rather than hindrance. In return for a large income, he would use his fleet against the Dutch and restore the Roman Catholic religion in England when the time was ripe.

However, at sea the Dutch were a match for the English, and on land, William, Prince of Orange, checked the French armies.

Through lack of money, Charles had to withdraw from the arena but continued on good terms with Louis.

He knew of the bitterness against the Roman Catholic faith in England and did not admit his faith until his deathbed. He had been a bad king.

The one good thing that happened during his reign was the passing of the Habeas Corpus Act. This meant that everyone had a right to a trial, so that they could either be punished or set free – not just left in jail at the king's pleasure.

James II 1685–1688

THREE YEARS

Charles II left no heir. His brother James, Duke of York, became king.

James II, like his brother, was a Catholic, but unlike his brother, did not keep his beliefs to himself. He favoured the Catholics.

A Protestant plan to overthrow James was formed in Holland. The leaders were the Earl of Argyll and the Duke of Monmouth.

Argyll tried in Scotland but his challenge was a failure. He was beaten and executed.

The Monmouth rebellion of 1685 started in the south-west of England and was a more serious threat. Thousands of Protestants supported him but they were not suitably armed.

At Sedgemoor, the Royal army beat the rebels. Monmouth was later executed. The king sent Judge Jeffreys to the West Country, and at the Bloody Assizes, more than 300 people were put to death. Hundreds of others were sent into slavery in the West Indies.

James announced a Declaration of Indulgence. This abolished the laws against people who were not Church of England. The clergy were ordered to read this declaration in every church. Most refused and seven bishops petitioned against the king. They were accused of rebellion, imprisoned and then tried.

The country was incensed by this, and a jury found the bishops not guilty.

At this time an invitation was sent to William of Orange in Holland to come and rule England. In doing so, he would preserve the liberties of the Protestant religion.

William of Orange was married to James II's daughter, Mary; his other daughter was Anne. Both were Protestants.

James II's overthrow was precipitated by the trial of the Seven Bishops.

When James II's first wife died he married an Italian noblewoman. They had a son.

It was rumoured that the baby was smuggled into the palace. Nevertheless there would be a line of Catholic monarchs unless something was done by the Protestants.

They invited William of Orange who had landed at Torbay in Devon and advanced cautiously.

Lord John Churchill went over to William's camp, as did Anne. With this news James II fled. He was captured but allowed to escape again.

His sole gesture of defiance was to drop the Great Seal into the Thames as he rowed away,

The Glorious Revolution, deposing James and establishing William, was over without a blow being struck.

William III 1688–1702 and Mary II 1688–1694

FOURTEEN YEARS

William's mother was English, the sister of James II. He was married to James II's daughter, Mary.

He didn't like England, but became king to help protect Holland from Louis XIV of France.

William and Mary were made joint sovereigns.

After his wife's death from smallpox, he became William III.

The English did not like 'Dutch Billy', but he needed England, and England needed a Protestant.

He was also known as William of Orange, and in time he became respected.

He had to deal with uprisings in both Scotland and Ireland.

William sent General Mackay to put down the Viscount Dundee, who had raised the Highlanders to support James II. In the Battle of Killiecrankie, the Scots beat the English, but Dundee was killed. Without a leader, the Scots drifted back to the glens.

In Ireland, James II arrived with money given by Louis XIV. The Irish agreed to help in order to get rid of their Protestant landlords.

The Irish besieged Londonderry for 105 days before it was relieved.

At this point William landed and marched on Dublin.

James had drawn up an army on the banks of the

Boyne.

William attacked, James fled to France and the English won the Battle of the Boyne (1690).

Peace was made on the understanding that Irish Catholics could have decent liberty. They were still treated harshly, however.

In Scotland, a pardon was offered to all who had fought William, if they took an oath of loyalty.

All the chiefs took this except the chief of the MacDonalds of Glencoe. He delayed his oath, arrived late at Fort William, but eventually took the oath six days later.

The MacDonalds were hated by Sir John Dalrymple (the king's advisor) and by the Campbells.

Dalrymple obtained permission to punish the MacDonalds for their delay.

In February 1692, he sent 120 Campbells to Glencoe. The MacDonalds showed them hospitality and billeted their guests for about one week.

Then one morning, the Campbells massacred the MacDonalds in their beds.

The crime was pinned unfairly on William, who surely did not realise the severity of Dalrymple's intentions.

The incident kept alive the Highland hatred of English rule, despite the fact that it was one Scottish clan that had slaughtered another.

At the same time, Louis XIV was planning an offensive.

William beat the French at sea and held them on land in the Netherlands.

It then seemed that, through marriage, France and Spain would unite and thereby dominate Europe. This was bad news for the Protestants.

At this time, William died from a riding accident.

He was succeeded by his wife's sister, Anne (the second daughter of James II).

William III was a good king, but not loved by his subjects.

Anne 1702–1714

TWELVE YEARS

Anne was an amiable woman whose husband, George of Denmark, played no part in British affairs.

She was entirely under the influence of Sarah Churchill (Duchess of Marlborough).

Sarah saw to it that her husband, John Churchill, The Duke of Marlborough, was made Commander of the Army.

The Churchills practically ruled the country.

Marlborough was probably the greatest soldier in British history. He cared for his men and was known as 'Corporal John'.

He forced back the French in the Netherlands, then rushed to Austria to save Vienna.

There followed a great victory at Blenheim, which changed the course of the war against the French.

This resulted in parliament gifting the magnificent Blenheim Palace to Marlborough as a token of their esteem.

The French were demoralised at the mention of his name. They were beaten to their knees, and then Marlborough, the great general who had never lost a battle or failed to take a fortress, was dismissed from his command in disgrace. This was caused because Sarah's perpetual tantrums caused her to lose the hold she had over the queen.

Mrs Masham came between her cousin Sarah and the queen, and promoted the break-up.

Sarah was dismissed from Court, and the Duke of Marlborough's fall followed.

The war with France was brought to an end. It was marked by the Treaty of Utrecht in 1713.

Britain gained Gibraltar and part of Canada.

Union with Scotland had occurred in 1707 to make the United Kingdom.

Scotland retained its own law courts and church.

This union was accelerated by Scotland's financial failure in the Darien Scheme (Panama).

All Anne's children died.

She wanted her brother, James Edward Stuart, to succeed her, but he was a Catholic and wouldn't change his religion.

Parliament and the people wanted a Protestant, and found one in George I of Hanover. He was the great-grandson of James I.

He was invited to take the crown.

George I 1714–1727

THIRTEEN YEARS

George I spoke no English, so Parliament ruled the country without interference.

He was a stout, plain man with no majesty.

He hated his oldest son.

George shut his own wife in a castle for life.

The Hanoverians were not popular.

The Stuart supporters (the Jacobites) tried to recover the throne.

In 1715 the Earl of Mar organised a gathering of the clans.

The standard of James VIII (the Pretender) was raised.

Mar was a poor general and wasn't able to take Edinburgh.

Eventually they fought the government's troops under Argyll at Sheriffmuir.

The Battle of Sheriffmuir was not decisive.

James Edward Stuart arrived late from France, and with no help, since Louis of France had died.

The 'fifteen' rising collapsed.

The Pretender and Mar went into exile.

Sir Robert Walpole became the country's Chief Minister during the reign. He was a wealthy landowner from Norfolk.

He believed in peace and quiet. This policy was later called 'laissez-faire'.

He kept taxes low and encouraged trade.

The country then had twenty years of peace.

George II 1727–1760

THIRTY-THREE YEARS

George disliked Walpole, but Queen Caroline persuaded him to keep Walpole in power.

Walpole became unpopular. By cunning and bribery he kept everything under his own control.

War broke out against France and Spain.

It went badly as Walpole had not reinvested in the navy and army.

George went to protect Hanover.

The Battle of Dettingen was the last battle in which an English king took command.

He won the battle, but his son lost the Battle of Fontenoy two years later in 1745.

The new Jacobite leader was Charles Edward (son of the old Pretender).

He was hoping to capitalise on the war in Europe. The French invasion fleet, however, was scattered by storms.

Known as Bonnie Prince Charlie, Charles Edward landed in Scotland and asked the clansman to follow him. The Jacobite army grew.

Bonnie Prince Charlie held Court at Holyrood, winning the hearts of all who met him.

They waited for a general uprising of support.

The delay allowed the government army to return from the continent.

In November 1745, the Jacobite march on England began. They took Carlisle and went as far as Derby. London was in a panic but the Jacobites lost motivation.

They turned round to go back, and made it to Scotland, but were soundly beaten at Culloden Moor by Cumberland's army.

All resistance was crushed with bloodthirsty cruelty. The 'forty-five' rebellion was over.

There was £30,000 on Charles's head but he was never betrayed while trying to escape.

Flora Macdonald once disguised him as 'Betty Burke', her Irish maid, to effect an escape.

Eventually he got a boat to France.

He later died a drunkard, in Rome.

The Jacobite cause then also died.

During this time, British trade was increasing. The trading companies included:

* The Africa Company
* The Levant Company (in the Mediterranean)
* The Hudson's Bay Company
* The East India Company

In India the rivalry was fierce. There was no strong government in India – just a number of warring princes.

The Europeans built forts and enlisted local troops to defend their warehouses.

The English or French Governor, with trained troops under European officers, could be very powerful in playing off one prince against another.

The French, under Governor Dupleix, gained control of most of the south of India.

They were about to end the British influence, when Robert Clive arrived. He was a clerk who turned to soldiering.

He was taken prisoner by the French in Madras but escaped.

Clive joined the East India Company Force and volunteered to attack Arcot – capital of the French-controlled province. He attacked and took Arcot with only a few troops.

This also helped Trichinopoly (a British interest) survive its siege by the French, since the latter had to withdraw troops to Arcot.

British prestige rose, and Dupleix was sent home in disgrace.

Clive returned to England with a fortune.

At this period, England was hard-pressed in Europe, America and India.

Admiral Byng was executed on his own quarterdeck for losing Minorca.

General Montcalm seemed certain to take Canada for France.

These disasters brought William Pitt to power as Prime Minister.

George II detested Pitt but recognised his popularity and talent.

Pitt picked good commanders who then hit back at the French. He improved the army and navy and financially supported Frederick the Great of Prussia.

Clive had returned to India.

Surajah Dowlah, who supported the French, captured the British post of Calcutta. 146 prisoners were put in a room called the Black Hole. All but twenty-three died by the next morning.

Clive came from Madras and recaptured the post of Calcutta. He then, with a small army, completely routed Dowlah at the Battle of Plassey (1757).

In the next three years Clive destroyed all traces of the French in India.

At this time, James Wolfe came to prominence and was promoted to General by Pitt. He had previously fought at Dettingen and Culloden.

Wolfe was sent to capture Louisbourg in Canada. This he did and then was ordered to take Quebec.

This was French held and positioned high on the St Lawrence River. Montcalm was the defending general. Wolfe became ill but masterminded a strategy.

The British took Quebec in 1759, but Wolfe and Montcalm were both killed. Britain then controlled all of Canada.

Also in 1759, England helped win the victory at Minden, which saved Frederick the Great.

Also, Admirals Boscawen and Hawke defeated the French at sea and averted an invasion.

George II died suddenly on the toilet while suffering from constipation.

George III 1760–1820

SIXTY YEARS

George III ended the Seven Years War and gained handsomely.

Frederick of Prussia never forgave George for leaving him in the lurch.

Pitt was sidelined as the Earl of Chatham.

In 1769 Captain Cook landed in New Zealand. (By 1837, there were still only about 2,000 whites in New Zealand – most were British.)

In 1770 he landed in Botany Bay in Australia. He called the area New South Wales.

The War of American independence took place. This was primarily between England and the English colonists. It was precipitated by the Boston Tea Party and by George demanding tax from the colonists. Independence was declared on 4 July 1776.

A man such as Wolfe or Clive would have won this war easily, but no such man was available.

Britain lost the thirteen American colonies and Minorca.

After Britain lost America as a colony and as a place where criminals could be sent, it was decided to use Australia as a convict colony.

It was hoped that free men would also go there to live and work so that it would become a colony like America had earlier been.

Captain Phillip was the first Governor of the new colony, based in Sydney. A few years later, free settlers arrived to farm land and create a land of plenty.

The Whigs took over in England.

George eventually got rid of them by dissolving Parliament. He appointed as Prime Minister William Pitt the younger, who was twenty-four. He held office for twenty years.

The Industrial Revolution gained momentum during this time. It created great wealth for both England and the new industrialists. England led the industrial world for the next one hundred years.

- John Kay invented the flying shuttle.
- James Hargreaves invented the spinning jenny.
- Richard Arkwright invented the spinning frame.
- James Watt and Matthew Walton improved the steam engine.
- The Reverend Edmund Cartwright invented the power loom.
- John Wilkinson developed the iron trade.
- James Brindley built canals for the Duke of Bridgewater.

The new urban areas produced terrible slums. The conditions of the poor were terrible but not as bad as they were in France.

The French Revolution occurred in 1789. King Louis XVI and Marie Antoinette were executed as a result. France was ruled by different power groups who were encouraging international revolution.

War broke out between England and France.

At the British naval attack on Toulon, Napoleon Bonaparte came to prominence. He was a Corsican of Italian descent who had attended military college.

War, and the absence of aristocrats, gave him the chance to rise. By twenty-six he was a general.

He defeated Italy and Austria and set his sights on

Egypt.

Admiral Nelson sailed into Aboukir Bay and destroyed his fleet.

Napoleon returned to Paris and overthrew the government. He became First Consul and then Emperor. He restored the fortunes of France. He quickly dominated Europe, but now needed to conquer England to complete his domination.

England stood alone.

In 1801 the first Imperial Parliament was called, with English, Welsh, Irish and Scottish members sitting together in the same House and making laws for the whole land.

Could England retain her naval supremacy?

Lord Nelson in the *Victory* thrashed the French fleet at the Battle of Trafalgar in 1805.

Nelson had already lost an eye and an arm in service.

During this battle Nelson lost 450 men, while the French, under Villeneuve, lost 5,000 men.

His last famous message for his fleet was, 'England expects that every man will do his duty.'

Trafalgar was the greatest British victory of all time. It brought command of the seas for a century and it made certain that Britain would not fall to Napoleon.

Nelson was killed during the battle.

Fighting continued against the French on Portuguese and Spanish soil. There emerged Arthur Wellesley (later to become the Duke of Wellington), known as 'Old Nosey'. He was not loved like Marlborough and Nelson, but he was trusted.

In 1812 Napoleon attempted to take Russia. He reached Moscow but had to retreat because of winter. His army perished in the snow and the French turned on Napoleon. He abdicated and was sent into exile on the isle of Elba.

After one year in exile, Napoleon escaped to France

and received a hero's welcome.

The allies, who had disbanded their forces, scraped an army together under Wellington's command.

The army of 80,000 was positioned in Belgium. About half were British. The rest were Dutch, Belgian and German. In addition, there were the Prussians (150,000) under Blücher, whom Wellington trusted. There was also an army of Russians and Austrians.

Napoleon defeated Blücher and then came on to deal with Wellington at Waterloo. It was a very gruelling, hard-fought battle. Eventually Blücher turned up again with the Prussians to help Wellington. Napoleon's Imperial Guard made a last effort but were beaten back and routed.

Napoleon surrendered, blaming Marshal Ney's cavalry tactics. He was exiled to St Helena where he died six years later.

The Battle of Waterloo was in 1815.

George III went blind and became mad for the last eight years of his reign.

In 1810, his son became Prince Regent; hence the Regency period.

George IV 1820–1830

TEN YEARS

George IV was the Prince Regent at the age of forty-eight (1812–1820).

He became known for his excesses – food, drink, gambling and women.

He became very obese and unsightly.

He married a Roman Catholic named Mrs Fitzherbert. The marriage was null and void from the start.

He then married Caroline of Brunswick (1795) in order to get Parliament to write off his debts.

After the birth of his daughter Charlotte, he separated from Caroline.

Caroline went to Italy, where she had several affairs. She returned to claim the crown in 1820.

After a trial it was decided the marriage was void and she should not be queen.

George was witty and very well versed in the arts.

He had great taste, set the fashion and was a man of style.

His close friend was George (Beau) Brummell.

He was responsible for the building of the Brighton Pavilion.

He made many promises to the Whigs, but always let them down.

Later in life, George became a recluse in Windsor Castle, surrounded by his former mistresses.

He could have been a much greater monarch, but he did not utilise his latent talents.

George Stephenson invented the *Rocket* during this reign, a railway engine which transformed not only industry, but the whole country.

George IV passed the Catholic Emancipation Act. This meant that Catholics could take seats in parliament or hold other public office, although it remained that no king can rule in England unless he is a Protestant.

He was not a good king.

William IV 1830–1837

SEVEN YEARS

William IV was the brother of the late King George IV. He had not expected to be king and was not groomed for it.

He was sent to sea at the age of thirteen.

William became very nautical and was known for his swearing and spitting in public.

He was George III's third son and was sixty-five when he became king. He was known as 'Silly Billy' and was regarded as an amiable fool.

His mistress was Mrs Jordan, with whom he had ten children.

He was opposed to the abolition of the slave trade, which was proposed by William Wilberforce and had been achieved in 1807 during the reign of George III.

Then in 1834, because of a government compensation package, most of the slaves in the West Indies were set free.

He married Adelaide, but they had no surviving children and therefore William had no heir.

He became quite eccentric.

He supported Catholic Emancipation.

William was very fit compared with his brother, George. He revelled in being king and could not conceal his pleasure. He showed considerable ability.

1830:   A Whig government, under Lord Grey, took over.

1831:   Re-election of the Whigs.

1832:   The Reform Bill was passed. This steered England away from revolution by reforming the representation of the people in Parliament.

1834:   William dismissed the Whigs and asked Peel, of the Conservatives, to be Prime Minister.

William wanted reform, but he wanted it steadily, not rapidly. This didn't work and he had to ask the Whigs to form a government.

William had a bad relationship with Victoria's mother. Because of this he hardly knew Victoria, his niece and heir to the throne.

Victoria 1837–1901

SIXTY-FOUR YEARS

Victoria was the niece of William IV.

Trade picked up and the railways continued to expand.

Britain exported more than all other nations put together.

The empire was growing bigger and richer.

Lord Palmerston was Premier.

Victoria was eighteen when crowned and shortly afterwards in 1840 married Prince Albert, her German cousin, with whom she had 9 children.

He was never popular but the marriage was very successful.

The Court became respectable and dull.

Albert died young in 1861 and Victoria retired into deep mourning. She was later coaxed into public life by Disraeli.

Her reign was successful and earned great respect for the Royal Family.

The Corn Laws

The Corn Laws protected English farmers by keeping the price of corn very high. This was done by stopping cheap imports. The results were starvation and poverty for the poor. The Corn Laws needed repealing.

At the same time, the poor people in Ireland lived largely on potatoes. Disease struck the potatoes, which resulted in the devastating effects of the Potato Famine in

1844–1848.

The Corn Laws were repealed, but it was too little, too late. Nearly 30% of the Irish died in the famine.

1848:   Known as 'the Year of Revolutions' in Europe. England escaped this violence and chaos.

1851:   The Great Exhibition was held in the Crystal Palace, which was erected from glass and iron, in Hyde Park. This was Prince Albert's project and drew people and exhibits from all over the world. It was a great success.

The Crimean War, 1854–1856

The Crimean War was fought to prevent Russia overthrowing the Turkish Empire.

The British and the French tried to take the Black Sea port of Sebastopol. The British troops were ill-equipped with summer gear, and medical treatment was atrocious.

Because of the invention of the electric telegraph, people had up-to-date reports of the war. They heard of the Battles of Alma and Inkerman. They heard of the brave but useless Charge of the Light Brigade, at Balaclava, where 607 men died.

The Earls of Cardigan and Raglan were prominent military leaders during the campaign.

Public indignation caused Florence Nightingale to be sent out to organise the medical treatment of wounded soldiers.

It was unusual for a high-born lady to be involved in nursing. She transformed the hospital base at Scutari in Turkey, although the army officers obstructed her.

She had thirty-eight nurses for help. She improved the food, the hygiene and the medical attention. The troops were devoted to her.

Florence transformed hospitals and the nursing profession. She, and Elizabeth Garret Anderson (first female doctor), made it possible for women to have both education and careers.

The Russians were defeated.

The Indian Mutiny, 1857

The Indian Mutiny affected only a small part of India.
It was caused by religion.

The army contained many Indian soldiers (sepoys). They were issued with a new Enfield rifle and cartridge which was coated with grease, which they had to bite before firing. Rumour had it the grease was:

1. Made from the fat of cows (sacred to Hindus); or
2. Made from the fat of pigs (unclean to Muslims).

This rumour, together with a prophecy that British rule would finish that year after one hundred years, provoked mutiny.

At Meerut the sepoys killed their officers.

They laid siege to Delhi, Cawnpore and Lucknow.

At Cawnpore a massacre took place and all the British colonists were killed.

The other two cities held out till help arrived. The whole province was then subdued.

As a result of the mutiny, the East India Company lost its powers and was taken over by the British Government. The queen appointed a Viceroy to rule in her absence.

India settled down for the next ninety years.

Livingstone in Africa

David Livingstone was born into a working-class background. He qualified as a doctor and became a missionary.

- He crossed the Kalahari Desert.
- He went to the Zambezi River.
- He discovered the Victoria Falls.
- He mapped a great area of Africa and returned to England a hero.
- He made two more trips taking in the Congo and Lake Tanganyika. It was the centre of the Arab slave trade.

After no news of him for four years, an American newspaper sent out an expedition to find him. This was headed by H M Stanley, the son of a Welsh prostitute.

He found Livingstone and was quoted as having said, 'Dr Livingstone, I presume?'

Livingstone then went on to his next trip, during which he died.

His heart was buried by Lake Bangweulu and his body in Westminster Abbey.

In the South, the Boers (Dutch settlers) resented British rule. They left the Cape Colony and trekked north to form the Boer republics of the Transvaal and the Orange Free State.

They were spread out in farms and couldn't control the warlike Zulus.

The Boers had to accept British annexation of the Transvaal. Eventually the Zulus were controlled and the Boers wanted their independence. This was granted by Mr Gladstone of the Liberals.

In England two of the most important political figures were Gladstone and Disraeli.

These two were always opposed and battling against each other.

Disraeli

He was the leader of the Conservatives.

He was Jewish.

He came from a humble background.

He wore flamboyant clothes.

He had a big curl on his forehead.

He had a venomous wit.

He was an eloquent speaker.

He rebuilt the Conservative Party after Peel fell from office.

He won Victoria's confidence and pulled her back into public life.

Victoria fell for his charms.

He made Victoria Empress of India.

He bought the Suez Canal for Britain.

Gladstone

He was Leader of the Liberals.

He was never at ease with the queen.

He always lectured her, so she disliked him.

He believed in reform, progress, peace abroad and justice for weaker nations.

He wanted the Irish to have Home Rule.

He was against expansion of the Empire.

He restored independence to the Boers.

The Boer War 1899–1902

Gold was discovered in the Transvaal (a Boer republic). As a result, Johannesburg sprang up overnight.

The newcomers were mostly British and soon outnumbered the Boers.

Paul Kruger, the Boer leader, wouldn't give them the right to vote and levied heavy taxes.

Cecil Rhodes came from Great Britain and made great wealth from the diamond mines of South Africa.

He wanted Southern Africa to be controlled by the

British, not the Boers. He despised the Boers.

He was Prime Minister of the Cape Colony and extended this to the Boer republics. He also formed a company to develop a large area of land north of the Transvaal.

This became Rhodesia.

The railway linked the Cape and Rhodesia.

The Boers were suspicious of being surrounded by Rhodes and his men.

Rhodes and his friend Dr Jameson concocted a plan to arrange an uprising of the British in Johannesburg.

The Jameson Raid was a terrible failure. It put an end to Rhodes' political career and inflamed the feeling between the British and the Boers.

With German weapons, the Boers attacked the British territories, and enjoyed great early success. They failed to follow this up, despite their advantage of numbers and weapons.

Instead of sweeping through to the Cape, they besieged Kimberley, Mafeking and Ladysmith. Colonel Baden-Powell was in command of Mafeking.

The towns were relieved by Lord Roberts and Lord Kitchener.

Pretoria, the Boer capital, was taken. Kruger became a fugitive.

The Boers wouldn't surrender, however. Guerrilla war was continued by Botha, De Wet and Smuts.

Eventually, Kitchener destroyed the Boer farms and put their families into concentration camps. History has been very critical of this treatment of the Boers.

Peace was eventually made and the Boer Republics re-established.

The union of South Africa was born in 1910.

★

Charles Dickens (1812–1870) rose to prominence as an author during this reign.

His works were fascinating social chronicles of the times.

Victoria reigned over the largest empire the world had ever seen.

During her reign, across the Atlantic, America experienced momentous change. This was caused by the impact of the American Civil War (1861–1865), which saw a massive step in the evolution of that country.

It also saw the abolition of slavery in America in 1865.

In 1867, the last convict ship was sent to Australia.

In 1900, the English Labour Party was formed.

Edward VII 1901–1910

As this point the British Empire covered 20% of the planet's land surface and was the biggest empire the world had ever known.

Edward was the son of Victoria.

She had denied him responsibilities, despite his lack of youth.

He liked racehorses and pretty women.

He took up his duties with surprising dignity.

In 1904 Britain and France signed the Entente Cordiale (Friendly Relationship).

The motor car was invented. By 1910 there were over 10,000 cars registered in Britain.

The Wright Brothers invented the aeroplane.

Also invented were tramcars, underground trains, movies, gramophones, radio sets and X-rays.

The first purpose-built cinema in England was built in 1907. The Picturedrome in Northampton (owned by this author) was built in 1912.

Shackleton and Scott went to the Antarctic.

Conditions improved for the industrial workers because of the Liberal Government led by Asquith in 1906.

They introduced:

- Old-age pensions;
- Unemployment pay;
- Sick benefits;

- Labour exchanges;
- Free school meals for the poor;
- A limited working week;
- Medical inspections in schools.

Asquith had two important ministers:

1. David Lloyd George, who came from a poor Welsh background.
2. Winston Churchill, who came from an aristocratic background.

In 1909 Lloyd George presented his 'People's Budget'.

It was defeated by the House of Lords. This had important consequences.

When Germany expanded her navy to threaten ours, the government ordered the construction of several up-to-date warships, the Dreadnoughts.

Early in this reign, Seebohm Rowntree and Charles Booth published their findings on city poverty. This poverty was totally unacceptable and stimulated the beginnings of the Welfare State.

Membership of the trade unions grew steadily.

1910 saw the first union strike.

George V 1910–1936

TWENTY–SIX YEARS

George was the second son of King Edward VII.

He changed the name of the Royal House from Saxe-Coburg-Gotha to Windsor.

He was therefore the first monarch belonging to the House of Windsor.

He served actively in the Royal Navy.

His older brother, Albert Victor, died of pneumonia, leaving George likely to succeed his father.

His marriage was arranged to Albert Victor's fiancée, Mary.[2] The marriage was a success, and unlike his father, George reportedly did not take a mistress.

Throughout their lives the couple exchanged notes of endearment and loving letters.

In contrast to his parents, George preferred a simple, almost quiet life.

When George became king, his wife became Queen Mary.

1911:   The Parliament Act limited the power of the Lords for good.

1912:   The *Titanic* sank off Newfoundland.

The 1914–1918 war, known as World War I, was triggered by the murder of Archduke Ferdinand of Austria in Sarajevo by a Serbian student. Austria threatened Serbia

---

2   Princess Victoria Mary of Teck, known as May.

and the murder was a convenient excuse. This caused two sides to develop:

The Allies	The Central Powers
Serbia	Austria-Hungary
Russia	Germany
France	Turkey (The Ottoman Empire)
Britain	Bulgaria

The real problem was the expansionist plans of Germany, who so far had no empire because of the busy empire building of the British and the French, and because Germany hadn't become a nation till 1871.

The German plan was to sweep through Belgium and take France before Russia could react.

Britain was regarded as no problem because she was only strong at sea.

Belgium was neutral territory and its invasion by Germany incensed the British.

The war started as a result of this invasion of Belgium, and by the end of it, 10 million soldiers had died.

By the end of 1914, the Western Front stretched 700 km from the English Channel to Switzerland. The two sides had dug themselves into parallel lines of trenches.

In the meantime the Russians attacked the Central Powers along the Eastern Front, which ran the length of the Russian border with Germany and Austria-Hungary.

It was a new type of warfare. The heavy artillery and machine-gun fire forced the troops to use trenches.

Trench warfare developed.

This caused absolute deadlock. Many lives were lost trying to break the deadlock.

The Germans used poisonous gas.

The Allies used tanks for the first time.

Aeroplanes were used for scouting and bombing for the first time. It was in this arena that William Barnard Rhodes Moorhouse (a previous resident of Spratton Grange whose governess had been Emily Wilding Davison), lost his life and became the first ever airman to receive the Victoria Cross.

Submarines were used for the first time.

Other nations joined the war. Italy and Romania joined the Allies.

Important battles on the Western Front included the Battles of the Marne, Ypres, the Somme and Vimy Ridge.

The Russians were very badly equipped. This caused Lloyd George and Churchill to decide to attack through the Balkans.

It was Churchill's plan to capture Constantinople (now Istanbul).

The naval attack on the Dardanelles failed. So did the Battle of Gallipoli.

As a result, Churchill left the Government to go soldiering in France.

In summary, Churchill fell from power, Asquith faded and Lloyd George came to power.

The war was going badly.

The German fleet was brought to the Battle of Jutland, but escaped into darkness after a large-scale skirmish. Soon after this Lord Kitchener was drowned at sea.

Lloyd George provided the leadership the country needed. The generals, including Haig (Commander-in-Chief) didn't like him, however. He was vain and tricky.

Admiral Beattie was well thought of.

T E Lawrence aided the Arab revolt against the Turks, although it was General Allenby who actually beat them.

Russia collapsed on the Eastern Front. This strengthened the German troops on the Western Front. As a result of this they nearly took Paris.

The USA joined the war in 1917 after the sinking of

the British ship the *Lusitania*.

The Allies under Marshal Foch held out as increasing numbers of Americans arrived.

Foch and Haig eventually broke the Germans.

Austria, Turkey and Bulgaria collapsed and the German fleet mutinied.

Civilians rioted in Germany and the Kaiser fled to Holland.

The war was over in 1918 and there followed the Treaty of Versailles, which was punitive to Germany.

A separate treaty broke up the Ottoman Empire.

The ending of World War I completely redrew the map of Europe. As boundaries changed, new countries emerged out of old empires.

The eleventh hour of the eleventh day of the eleventh month is used annually to commemorate the ending of the war on Armistice Day.

The League of Nations was created to prevent further wars. It was later replaced by the UN.

World War I was a difficult time for the Royal Family as they had many German relatives.

Kaiser Wilhelm of Germany was the king's first cousin and was known as 'Willy' within the family.

George V and Tsar Nicholas II of Russia were first cousins. Their mothers were sisters.

When Nicholas was overthrown in the Russian Revolution of 1917, the British Government offered asylum to the Tsar and his family. Because of worsening conditions for the British people, and fears that revolution might spread, George decided that the presence of the Romanovs was not appropriate. He therefore opposed the rescue.

The Tsar and his immediate family remained in Russia and were murdered by the Bolshevik revolutionaries in Yekaterinburg in 1918.

During World War I, many of the monarchies which

had ruled Europe fell.

In 1922, a Royal Navy ship was sent to Greece to rescue George's cousins and their children. This included Prince Philip, who would later marry George's granddaughter, Elizabeth II.

The years that followed the war were hard and there was high unemployment throughout Europe.

Lloyd George slid from power and even higher unemployment followed (30%).

There was no real national leader.

In 1926 there was a General Strike which lasted nine days. It had a devastating effect on the country.

During the General Strike, the king took exception to suggestions that the strikers were revolutionaries. He also advised the Government against taking inflammatory action.

The contenders for leadership included Stanley Baldwin and Ramsay MacDonald.

During this time England led the world in:

- Aircraft manufacture
- Civil aviation
- Car racing
- Most sports

1928: The vote was given to all women over the age of twenty-one. This was after years of campaigning by the Suffragette Movement whose leaders included Emmeline Pankhurst and Emily wilding Davison. The latter, who had lived at Spratton Grange near Northampton, had sacrificed her life in 1913 by throwing herself in front of the King's horse at the Epsom Derby.

1929:	The New York Stock Exchange crashed and precipitated the Great Depression.
1931/32:	Almost 3 million people were unemployed (22% of the workforce).
1932:	King George agreed to deliver a personal Christmas speech on the radio, an event that was to become annual. He had become a well-loved king.

Sadly, George's relationship with his heir, Prince Edward, deteriorated during these later years.

George was disappointed in Edwards's failure to settle down in life and was disgusted by his many affairs with married women.

He was reluctant to see Edward inherit the crown.

In contrast he was fond of his second eldest son, Prince Albert, who was known as 'Bertie' and later became King George VI.

He also doted on his eldest granddaughter, Princess Elizabeth, whom he nicknamed 'Lilibet', and who called him 'Grandpa England'.

George had a weak chest and was a heavy smoker.

After his death his physician admitted that he had hastened the king's demise by giving him a lethal injection of cocaine and morphine.

This was done to prevent further strain on the family, and so that news of his death could be announced in the morning edition of *The Times*.

At the lying in State, his four surviving sons mounted the guard at the catafalque on the last night.

One of his sons had died at the age of thirteen, from epilepsy.

His son George had been a reformed hard drug addict.

George V was buried at St George's Chapel, Windsor Castle.

Irish Politics

During the reign of George V, there was a large change in the relationship between Ireland and England.

Home Rule bills for Ireland introduced by Gladstone during Victoria's reign had been defeated, but a measure of local government was given.

In 1912 however, Asquith introduced his Home Rule Bill. It was passed in 1914 just before war broke out.

Because of the war, however, an act was passed to postpone it.

Sir Roger Casement then tried to bring German aid to Ireland. For this he was tried and hanged.

1916 was the year of the Easter Rebellion.

Rebels seized important buildings in Dublin and proclaimed Ireland a republic.

The fifteen leaders were tried and executed. These events were obviously very harmful to the relationship between the two countries.

Irish leadership fell more and more to Sinn Fein (Ourselves Alone), a revolutionary party which set up an Irish Parliament in 1919. It was dedicated to making Ireland an independent Republic. One of its main leaders was Eamon de Valera.

A new Home Rule Bill then proposed one parliament for Ulster and one for the rest of Ireland.

This was not acceptable to Sinn Fein but was signed by Michael Collins, believing it was the best deal for Ireland at the time.

In 1921, the Ulster Parliament opened as part of the UK.

In 1922, the Irish Free State was formed with full dominion status in the British Empire. Michael Collins was then assassinated in an ambush. He was accused of 'selling out'.

The British soldiers sent to Ireland to help the Royal

Irish Constabulary in 1920–1921 were known as the Black and Tans because of the colour of their uniform. They were hated by the Irish because of their ruthless attacks in revenge for IRA actions.

The Irish Free State was always at odds with Ulster over boundaries and political ideals.

Ireland was plunged into a Civil War known as The Troubles. This was between the Republicans who wanted independence and the Free Staters who accepted the Treaty.

Eamon de Valera and his party wanted a full republic, but accepted the Treaty in 1923.

During this time, there was great bitterness and many many casualties.

In 1932 de Valera rose to power and continued to aim at full independence.

In 1937, the Irish Free State became the independent sovereign state of Eire.

It was not till 1949 that Eire adopted the official name The Irish Republic, and in the same year left the Commonwealth.

Edward VIII 1936

Edward VIII was king for eleven months from the death of his father, George V, on 20 January 1936, until his abdication on 10 December 1936.

He was the second monarch of the House of Windsor.

When the First World War (1914–1918) broke out Edward joined the army.

He witnessed trench warfare at first hand and attempted to visit the front line as often as he could.

His role in the war, although limited, led to his great popularity among veterans of the conflict.

He soon became the 1920s version of a latter-day movie star. At the height of his popularity, he became the most photographed celebrity of his time, and he set men's fashion. The Windsor knot was named after his fondness for large-knotted ties.

King George V was disappointed in Edward's failure to settle down in life and disgusted by his many affairs with married women. He was reluctant to see Edward inherit the crown.

Edwards's attachment to Mrs Simpson further weakened his poor relationship with his father. Although the king and queen met Mrs Simpson at Buckingham Palace in 1935, they later refused to receive her. But Edward had now fallen in love with Wallis, and the couple grew even closer.

Edward VIII became the first Commonwealth monarch to fly in an aeroplane, when he flew from Sandringham to London for his Accession Council.

On 16 July 1936, an attempt was made on the king's life. An Irish journalist and malcontent, Jerome

Brannigan, produced a loaded revolver as the king rode on horseback at Constitution Hill, near Buckingham Palace. Police spotted the gun and pounced on him; he was quickly arrested.

On 16 November 1936, Edward invited Prime Minister Stanley Baldwin to Buckingham Palace and expressed his desire to marry the American divorcee, Wallis Simpson, when she became free to remarry. Baldwin informed the king that his subjects would deem the marriage morally unacceptable, largely because the Church opposed remarriage after divorce, and the people would not tolerate Wallis as queen.

On the night of 10 December 1936, Edward, now reverting to the title Prince Edward, made a broadcast to the nation and the Empire, explaining his decision to abdicate. He famously said, 'I have found it impossible to carry the heavy burden of responsibility, and to discharge my duties as king as I would wish to do, without the help and support of the woman I love.' Rather than give up Mrs Simpson, he chose to abdicate.

The new king, George VI announced he was to make his brother Duke of Windsor.

The king's decision to create Edward a Royal Duke ensured that he could neither stand for election to the House of Commons nor speak on political subjects in the House of Lords.

The Duke of Windsor married Mrs Simpson, in a private ceremony on 3 June 1937 in France.

His brother, now George VI, absolutely forbade members of the Royal Family to attend. This vendetta was instigated and continued by Queen Elizabeth, who was furious about the position her husband had been put into.

The denial of the style 'HRH' to the Duchess of Windsor caused conflict, as did the financial settlement. The government declined to include the Duke or the

Duchess on the Civil List, and the Duke's allowance was paid personally by the king.

Edward became embittered against his own mother.

In the early days of George VI's reign, the Duke telephoned daily, asking for money and requesting that the Duchess be granted the style of HRH, until the harassed king ordered that the calls not be put through.

The Duke had assumed that he would settle in Britain after a year or two of exile in France. However, King George VI (with the support of his mother, Queen Mary and his wife, Queen Elizabeth) threatened to cut off his allowance if he returned to Britain without an invitation. The new king and queen were also forced to pay Edward for Sandringham House and Balmoral Castle. These properties were Edward's personal property, inherited from his father, King George V, on his death, and thus did not automatically pass to George after the abdication.

In 1937, the Duke and Duchess visited Germany, against the advice of the British Government, and met the Nazi leader Adolf Hitler at Berchtesgaden. The visit was much publicised by the German media. During the visit the Duke gave full Nazi salutes.

The couple then settled in France.

In February 1940, the German Minister in The Hague, Count Zech, claimed that the Duke had leaked the Allied war plans for the defence of Belgium.

When Germany invaded the North of France in May 1940, the Windsors fled south, first to Biarritz, then in June to Spain. In July the pair moved to Lisbon, where they lived at first in the home of a banker with German contacts.

A 'defeatist' interview by the Duke that was widely distributed may have served as the last straw for the British Government. The Prime Minister, Winston Churchill, threatened the Duke with a court martial if he did not return to British soil.

In August, a British warship dispatched the pair to the Bahamas, where in the view of Winston Churchill, the Duke could do the least damage to the British war effort.

The Duke of Windsor was installed as Governor.

He held the post until the end of World War II in 1945.

Some believed that Edward favoured German fascism as a bulwark against communism, and even that he initially favoured an alliance with Germany.

Edward's experience of 'the unending scenes of horror' during World War I led him to support appeasement. Hitler considered Edward to be friendly towards Nazi Germany, saying, 'His abdication was a severe loss for us.'

Many historians have suggested that Hitler was prepared to reinstate Edward as king in the hope of establishing a fascist Britain.

It is widely believed that the Duke (and especially the Duchess) sympathised with fascism before and during World War II, and had to remain in the Bahamas to minimise their opportunities to act on those feelings.

During the occupation of France, the Duke asked the German forces to place guards at his Paris and Riviera homes: they did so.

After the war, the Duke admitted in his memoirs that he admired the Germans, but he denied being pro-Nazi. Of Hitler he wrote, 'The Führer struck me as a somewhat ridiculous figure, with his theatrical posturing and his bombastic pretensions.'

The couple returned once again to France.

Effectively taking on the role of minor celebrities, the couple were for a time in the 1950s and 1960s regarded as part of café society.

The Royal Family never accepted the Duchess and would not receive her formally, but the Duke sometimes met his mother and brother. Queen Mary in particular maintained her anger against Edward and her indignation regarding Wallis. 'To give up all this for that,' she said.

In 1965, the Duke and Duchess returned to London for a memorial ceremony for Queen Mary. They were visited by Queen Elizabeth.

The Duke died of throat cancer on the 28 May 1972, at his home in Paris, and his body was returned to Britain for a burial at Frogmore, near Windsor Castle. The increasingly senile and frail Duchess travelled to England to attend his funeral, staying at Buckingham Palace during her visit. She died fourteen years later, and was buried alongside her husband simply as 'Wallis, Duchess of Windsor'.

George VI 1936–1952

As the second son of King George V, George VI was not expected to inherit the throne, and spent his early life in the shadow of his elder brother, Edward.

As a child, the future George VI was known as Prince Albert.

He often suffered from ill health and was described as 'easily frightened and somewhat prone to tears'.

Albert developed a severe stammer that lasted for many years, as well as chronic stomach problems. He suffered from knock knees, and to correct this he was forced to wear splints, which were extremely painful. He was also forced to write with his right hand, although he was naturally left-handed.

He served in the navy during World War I, and after the war took on all the usual round of public engagements.

It was unusual, in a time when royals were expected to marry fellow royals, that Albert had a great deal of freedom in choosing a wife. In 1920 he met Lady Elizabeth Bowes-Lyon. He became determined to marry her.

Although Lady Elizabeth was a direct descendant of King Robert I of Scotland and King Henry VII of England, she was in British law a commoner.

She rejected his proposal twice and hesitated for nearly two years, reportedly because she was reluctant to make the sacrifices necessary to become a member of the Royal Family.

After a protracted courtship he married Elizabeth

Bowes-Lyon in 1923, and they had two daughters, Elizabeth (who later succeeded him as Queen Elizabeth II) and Margaret.

Albert's marriage to a British commoner was considered a modernising gesture.

Albert assumed the style and title 'King George VI' to emphasise continuity with his father and restore confidence in the monarchy.

George VI was also forced to buy the royal houses of Balmoral Castle and Sandringham House from Prince Edward, as these were private properties and did not pass to George on his accession.

The 1920s and 30s saw the growth of fascism in Europe.

This was fuelled by the punitive nature of the Treaty of Versailles (1919) and by the rise of socialism. German industrialists were fearful of left-wing politics and would back any alternative.

In 1933, Adolf Hitler's Nazi Party came to power in Germany, promising strong leadership and a restoration of national pride.

He began to build up the armed forces and to reclaim territories lost as a result of WWI.

The League of Nations was too weak to stop Hitler's aggression.

The growing likelihood of war erupting in Europe came to dominate the early reign of George VI. The king was constitutionally bound to support the Prime Minister, Neville Chamberlain, in his appeasement stance towards Adolf Hitler. When the king and queen greeted Chamberlain on his return from negotiating the Munich Agreement in 1938, they invited him to appear on the balcony of Buckingham Palace with them. This public association of the monarchy with a politician was exceptional, as balcony appearances were traditionally restricted to the Royal Family.

On 1 September 1939, Hitler invaded Poland.

France and Britain declared war on Germany on 3 September.

This was the beginning of World War II, with the Allies versus the Axis Powers (Germany and Italy).

The Germans quickly swept through Poland, Denmark, Norway, Belgium, The Netherlands and France.

In May 1940, the Allied forces were trapped and had to evacuate from the French port of Dunkerque across the English Channel.

When war broke out, George VI and his wife resolved to stay in London and not flee to Canada, as had been suggested. The king and queen officially stayed in Buckingham Palace throughout the war, although they usually spent the nights at Windsor Castle to avoid bombing raids.

George VI and Queen Elizabeth narrowly avoided death when two German bombs exploded in a courtyard at Buckingham Palace while they were there.

Throughout the war, the king and queen made morale-boosting visits throughout the UK, visiting bomb sites and munitions factories. The Royal Family adhered to rationing restrictions in the country at the time. Eleanor Roosevelt, during her stay at Buckingham Palace during the war commented on the rationed food served in the Palace, and the limited bathwater that was permitted.

In 1940, Neville Chamberlain lost the support of the House of Commons and was replaced as Prime Minister by Winston Churchill.

Significant events included:

1940:   Italy declared war on France and Britain.
Children were evacuated from the Blitz cities.
Food rationing was introduced.
The fascist leader, Benito Mussolini, sent Italian troops to confront Allied troops in North Africa.

The Allies' main priority was to keep the supply route open to the Suez Canal and the oilfields of the Middle East.

The Allies proved superior.

Japan joined the Axis Powers, Germany and Italy.

Japan wanted an empire in South East Asia, but to do so they had to destroy the American Pacific Fleet.

France surrendered to Germany in June.

The Battle of Britain was an air battle between the RAF and the Luftwaffe fought between July and September. The RAF were victorious.

The bombing Blitz on London and Coventry lasted during September and October.

London was bombed every night for fifty-eight nights.

1941: Clothes rationing was introduced.

The use of radar and sonar were powerful tools used during this war.

The German invasion of the USSR began.

Germany invaded Greece and Yugoslavia.

The Royal Navy sank the German battleship *Bismarck*.

Britain and the USA agreed the Atlantic Charter, pledging freedom of the seas.

Japan attacked the US fleet in Pearl Harbor, Hawaii.

Germany and Italy declared war on the USA.

All unmarried women between twenty and thirty years were conscripted either into the armed forces or into key industries.

Hitler sent specialist reinforcements to help the Italians in North Africa.

The German troops were under the respected leadership of General Rommel, who was known

as 'the Desert Fox'.
The Allies declared war on Japan.

1942:   The USA joined the Allies against Germany.
The United Nations declared they would not make separate peace deals with the Axis Powers.
The Allied bombing of Cologne: 900 bombers were used.
The Battle for Stalingrad began.
At the Battle of El Alamein, Allied troops under the command of Field Marshall Montgomery forced the Axis troops to retreat. Monty's troops were known as 'the Desert Rats'.
Singapore fell to Japan. 85,000 soldiers were taken prisoner.
At the Battle of the Coral Sea, the Allies checked the threat to Australia.
The Americans defeated the Japanese fleet at the Battle of Midway. This was the first major Allied victory against the Japanese.

1943:   Roosevelt and Churchill agreed to accept only unconditional surrender from the Axis.
German troops surrender in Stalingrad.
The Axis surrendered in North Africa. This gave the Allies a launch pad to attack Southern Europe.
The Allies invaded Sicily.
Italy surrendered to the Allies.
The Allies began to drive Japanese forces from the Pacific.

1944:   On 6 June, the Allied troops made the D-Day landings in Normandy under the overall command of the American General Eisenhower. This was the final offensive. They rapidly reached Paris. In the meantime, Soviet troops were advancing from the East, and Allied troops were moving north from the South of France.

There was a failed plot to assassinate Hitler.

Allied troops, and the Free French under the leadership of General de Gaulle, liberated Paris.

The Battle of the Bulge in Belgium formed the last German attack on the Allies.

1945:   Allied bombers destroy the German city of Dresden. 80,000 civilians were killed in one night.

As Soviet troops surrounded Berlin, Adolf Hitler committed suicide.

The Germans surrendered on 7 May.

8 May was declared VE (Victory in Europe) Day.

Belsen, the Nazi concentration camp, was revealed, together with the other horrors of the Jewish Holocaust.

At the Yalta Conference in Ukraine, Stalin, Roosevelt and Churchill decided the fate of Germany and spheres of influence in Europe.

Americans dropped the Atomic bomb on Hiroshima and Nagasaki in August in order to bring an end to the war with Japan.

Japan surrendered on 2 September – VJ Day.

The United Nations was formed.

1945–1949:   The trials of Nazi war criminals were held in Nuremburg. Several were sentenced to death and executed.

Although there were many theatres of war, some of the most brutal and devastating fighting was done on the Eastern Front between the Germans and the Soviets.

This is shown by the record of military losses for World War II:

USSR	13,600,000
Germany	3,300,000
British Empire	357,000 (UK 264,000)
USA	292,000

Some historians claim that it was the sacrifice made by Soviet troops which crippled the German war machine.

When the war was won in 1945, the king duly invited Churchill to appear with him on the balcony of Buckingham Palace for the VE Day celebrations.

After six years of war, the Empire was weakened. The United States and Soviet Union were the rising world powers.

Winston Churchill, despite his success, was replaced as Prime Minister by Clement Attlee, the Labour leader.

George VI's reign saw the acceleration of the break up of the British Empire and the creation and growth of the Commonwealth.

This had all begun during his father's reign with the Balfour Declaration in 1917. This was formalised in the Statute of Westminster in 1931. A timetable had been set out for the transition of countries into sovereign states over a period of years.

1946: Transjordan became independent as the Hashemite Kingdom of Jordan.

1947: Independence for India, which was divided into India and Pakistan.

1948: Independence for Burma and Ceylon (Sri Lanka).

1948: Independence for Palestine, although it was divided between Israel and the Arab states.

On achieving independence from the Empire, some countries decided to join the newly created Commonwealth. Some decided against this. (In 2000 there were fifty-one member states in the Commonwealth of Nations.)

1948:   Birth of the National Health Service (NHS) in the UK. This provides free medical services at the point of need.

1951:   The Festival of Britain was staged in London.

The war had taken its toll on the king's health. This was exacerbated by his heavy smoking and subsequent development of lung cancer. Increasingly, his daughter Princess Elizabeth, the heiress to the throne, took on more of the royal duties as her father's health deteriorated.

In the autumn of 1951, the king's cancerous lung was removed.

In January 1952, despite advice from those close to him, he went to the airport to see off Princess Elizabeth, who was going on a tour of Australia. It was the last time he would see her.

On 6 February 1952, George VI died in his sleep at Sandringham House in Norfolk, at the age fifty-six. He was interred in St George's Chapel in Windsor Castle.

In 2002, the body of his wife, Queen Elizabeth, and the ashes of his daughter, Princess Margaret, were interred in a chapel alongside him.

Significant Dates

55BC	Julius Caesar invaded Britain.
43AD	Claudius invaded Britain.
410	The approx date that the Romans left Britain .
449	The Saxons Hengist and Horsa arrived in Britain.
597	Augustine brought Christianity to England.
875	King Alfred defeated the Danes at sea.
1002	Ethelred instigated the slaughter of all Danes living in England.
1066	The Battle of Hastings/ The Norman Conquest
1086	Domesday Book completed.
1099	The First Crusade.
1172	Henry 11 invaded Ireland.
1215	Magna Carta.
1264	Simon de Montfort summons parliament.
1277	Edward 1 invaded Wales.
1290	Edward 1 expelled the Jews from England.
1295	The Model Parliament was set up.
1340	The start of the 100 years war against France.
1346	The Battle of Crecy.
1348	The Black Death.
1355	The Battle of Poitier.
1381	The Peasants Revolt.
1415	The Battle of Agincourt.
1453	The end of the Hundred Years War with France.

1455	The Battle of St Albans.
1455-85	The War of the Roses
1460	The Battle of Northampton.
1461	The Battle of Towton.
1485	The Battle of Bosworth Field.
1492	Christopher Columbus made his epic voyage.
1513	The Battle of Flodden.
1529	Henry V111 became the head of the Church of England
1555	The burning of Bishop Hooper and John Rogers at Smithfield.
1588	The Spanish Armada.
1605	The Gunpowder Plot
1611	The Printing of the St James Bible.
1620	The Puritans set sail in the Mayflower.
1628	The Petition of Right.
1642-51	The Civil War –Royalists v Roundheads.
1642	The Battle of Edgehill.
1644	The Battle of Marston Moor.
1645	The Battle of Naseby.
1649	The Execution of Charles 1.
1665	The Great Plague.
1666	The Great Fire of London.
1690	The Battle of the Boyne.
1692	The Massacre of Glencoe.
1704	Marlborough wins The Battle of Blenheim.
1707	The Act of Union between England and Scotland.
1713	The Treaty of Utrecht.
1715	The First Jacobite rebellion.
1745	The Second Jacobite rebellion.
1757	The Battle of Plassey.
1759	Wolfe died taking Quebec
1769	Captain Cook landed in New Zealand.

1770	Captain Cook landed in Botany Bay, Australia.
1776	American Independence.
1789	The French Revolution.
1805	The Battle of Trafalgar.
1807	Wilberforce's Abolition of Slavery.
1815	The Battle of Waterloo.
1844-48	The Irish Potato Famine.
1848	The Year of Revolutions in Europe.
1854-56	The Crimean War.
1857	The Indian Mutiny.
1861-65	The American Civil War.
1867	The Last convict ship sent to Australia.
1875	Britain bought the Suez Canal.
1899-1902	The Boer War.
1900	The English Labour Party was formed.
1904	The Entente Cordiale was signed.
1909	The Peoples Budget defeated by the Lords.
1910	The Union of South Africa was born.
1911	The Parliament Act.
1912	The Titanic sank.
1912	Asquith's Home Rule Bill for Ireland.
1914-18	World War 1.
1916	The Easter rebellion in Ireland.
1917	The Russian Revolution.
1918	The Treaty of Versailles.
1921	The Ulster Parliament opened as part of UK.
1922	The Irish Free State was formed.
1926	The General Strike.
1928	The vote was given to all women over 21 years.
1929	New York Wall Street stock exchange crashed.
1933	Adolf Hitler came to power.

1937	The Irish Free State became Eire.
1938	The Munich Agreement.
1939-45	World War 11.
1940	Dunkerque.
1940	The Battle of Britain.
1941	Germany invaded USSR.
1941	Pearl Harbour.
1942	The USA joined the Allies.
1944	The Normandy landings.
1945	Germany surrendered.
1945	Atomic bombs were dropped on Hiroshima and Nagasaki.
1945	Japan surrendered.
1945	The United Nations was formed.
1947	Independence for India which was partitioned into India and Pakistan.
1948	Independence for Burma and Ceylon(Sri Lanka)
1948	Independence for Palestine and the formation of the Jewish State.
1948	The Birth of the NHS.
1949	Eire became The Irish Republic.

Lightning Source UK Ltd.
Milton Keynes UK
UKOW04f0643210415

250012UK00001B/9/P

101

TRUTHS ABOUT DIVINE SUCCESS

MATTYSON MEDIA

MATTHEW ASHIMOLOWO

CONTENTS

Chapter One

(20) Truths About Vision

The difficulty many people have is not the need for dreams, rather, how to know which of the thousand and one ideas which cross their minds is really of God. It will be sad to get to eternity to discover that you have pursued someone else's vision and dream. So in this chapter, I will share twenty ways to know if a vision or dream or idea which you have is your God-given vision or one of the many good things which could come to your heart.

1. All God-given visions are revelatory in nature.

Joseph held on to his vision because it was not something he made up. It was revealed in the inner recess of his heart by the God of heaven. Having know that God put it in his heart, he could not shake it off, so he verbalized it. He looked for someone who believed in it and sought to achieve it.

God's revelatory vision does not only come by dreams in the night. It could be through the *still small voice* in you heart, *premonition, a vision* or *visual image*. It could be the *prophetic utterance* from you or someone else, a *Word of knowledge* or as in the case of Belteshazar, *words being written supernaturally*.

2. God-given visions are "compulsive in motivation".

Ten older brothers threw Joseph into a well. Slavery was an attack to kill whatever vision he had from God, though Joseph was a teenager when he had this revelation. Now as a mature adult he knew the vision he saw was God's divine destiny for his future. Instead of looking for an easy way out, the same vision which got him into danger was also his source of sustenance. The Lord Jesus Christ endured the cross and shame because of the glory set before him.

When your God-given vision is misunderstood, laughed at, questioned and thought to be too high for a person like you, there will be a compulsion which goes along with it. That compulsion will make you go on with the vision.

3. A God-given vision will be "outlasting in scope".

When we look through the scriptures from Genesis to Revelation, we see men and women whose visions and dreams extended beyond their generation.

In natural history, men who have left their footprints on the sands of time were people who had visions beyond their immediate time. Such men did not concentrate on where they were; their focus was on their destination. They found ways of building bridges which closed the gap from where they were to their destination.

4. "A strong desire."

When a vision is from God there will be a strong desire to make it happen, even if you cannot see how you will achieve it. Every major enterprise on earth, every major breakthrough only became a success story after it got transformed from a thought to a dream. Dreams become ideas, ideas turn to action and action to results. Everyone is interested in a success story. People do not remember the ten spies who brought the evil report.

Once you decide your direction, God will maintain your energy for the distance.

5.   A God-given vision is "satisfying".

You will be happy when you know where God wants you to be. The medical doctor who helps people to get well, the mechanic who finds satisfaction in making cars work, are on the same level when it comes to the fulfilment of dreams. The day may come, though, when one of them decides to go the extra mile in doing the job he chose as his career.

Henry Ford chose to go beyond repairing cars. He decided to make cars affordable to all men. He found fulfilment in making life comfortable for the commuter and others. Jesus said:

> *"The thief cometh not, but for to steal, and to kill, and to destroy: I am come that they might have life and that they might have it more abundantly."*
> *[John 10:10]*

this verse quoted means, of course, that whatever vision God has for your life is not small. God made you wonderful. You are too precious to be wasted material.

It is important for you to find out which of your ideas brings satisfaction, even at the mere thought of it. Pursue such an idea, until you achieve it.

Do not waste your future being dissatisfied with yourself every day. The same energy you expend measuring your enemy or problem, the same thought and strength you give to complaining about your life, is the same amount of time you have to pursue your God-given dream and know victory.

6. "All God-given dreams and visions are an investment and not an expenditure".

Joseph's life became an investment not a wasted life. Jesus' life was an investment. People in Scripture, the disciples, missionaries, preachers who have lived in our times, lived their lives as investments and not as expenditure.

Every day, as you and I walk the streets, we encounter people, we meet men and women for whom life is a mere expenditure. In most cases these people seem to be heading nowhere, they are part of the great crowd of humanity who may have concluded that the whole purpose of a man's life is to eat, drink and die.

Will you live a fulfilled life? Or contribute to the wealth of the grave?

7. "There are examples in scripture of men and women who knew why they were on earth and pursued that purpose."

One example, whose life has been quoted throughout this book is "Joseph".

He had a dream. The interpretation of his dream was that he would be a leader. The subsequent experiences were leading in the direction of the fulfilment of that dream. His life drives home the fact that if God gives you a vision and it is opposed by men, do not reduce your vision, but stay in the will of God. It shall come to pass.

Jeremiah:

> "Before I formed thee in the belly I knew thee; and before thou camest forth out of the womb I sanctified thee, and I ordained thee a prophet unto the nations. Then said I, Ah Lord God! Behold I cannot speak: for I am a child. But the Lord said unto me, Say not, I am a child: for thou shalt go to all that I shall send thee, and whatsoever I command thee thou shalt speak. Be not afraid of their faces: for I am with thee to deliver thee, saith the Lord. Then the Lord put forth his hand, and touched my mouth. And the Lord said unto me, Behold, I have put my words in thy mouth. See, I have this day set thee over the nations, and over the kingdoms, to root out, and to pull down, and to destroy, and to throw down, to build, and to plant."
> [Jeremiah 1: 5-10]

The literal meaning of the name Jeremiah is that *'God establishes, appoints or sends'*. Jeremiah received from the Lord a prophetic word that he had been ordained while he was in his mother's womb.

This shows that there was a purpose which Jeremiah was to fulfil. But like all other millions of people on earth, the visions, dreams, and God-given *redemptive revelations* may be missed if we choose to walk in our own will. We said earlier that some people are born original, but die as 'photocopies'. Having told Jeremiah that he had been chosen for a purpose God instructed him not to allow his youth, fear, faces or his lack of eloquence stop him from achieving his divine destiny. Having set him apart, God revealed to him what his calling was.

Though Jeremiah was a prophet, in the realm of the Spirit he had been set over nations, to root out and pull down strongholds, to destroy them and pull down, to build up and plant God's people.

> *"See I have this day set thee over the nations and over the kingdoms, to root out, and to pull down, and to destroy, and to throw down, to build, and to plant."*
> *[Jeremiah 1: 10]*

If he had moved out of God's will he would have missed it. Though Jeremiah was born at the time when the nation of Judah was being persuaded he did not lead a Civil Rights Movement. It was not his calling.

Paul:

In Acts 9: 15-16,

> *"But the Lord said unto him, Go thy way: for he is a chosen*

> *vessel unto me, to bear my name before the Gentiles, and*
> *kings, and the children of Israel: For I will shew he how*
> *great thing he must suffer for my name's sake."*
> *[Acts 9: 15-16]*

In the passage quoted Paul was to build a spiritual enterprise for God. He touched nations, he preached to kings, reached the intellectuals. He shared the message of Jesus Christ in the three popular languages of his time, Hebrew, Latin and Greek.

A citizen of Rome, having been born in Tarsus, his education in the legal system of the Jews, all worked together for the fulfilment of God's ultimate calling or style of Paul. If we look closely we see that Paul was persecuted and made to go through almost impossible situations, suffering excessively for the gospel. Despite shipwreck, scourging, false brethren and evil reports, he preached the gospel as a man who could not walk away from that one commission.

> *"Whom we preach, warning every man, and teaching*
> *every man in all wisdom; that we may present every man*
> *perfect in Christ Jesus." [Colossians 1: 28]*

Paul pursued and concluded the vision God gave him. In one of his books (which today has blessed us), he knew when his time came to leave the stage for others to propagate and perpetuate what he started.

"For I am now ready to be offered, and the time of my departure is at hand. I have fought a good fight, I have finished my course, I have kept the faith. Henceforth there is laid up for me a crown of righteousness, which the Lord, the righteous judge, shall give me at that day: and not to me only, but unto all them also that love his appearing." [2 Timothy 4: 6-8]

Jesus:

Lastly, Jesus, our Master and Saviour knew why he came to the world, and when he fulfilled his divine destiny, he knew it. We will be freaks of nature if we do not walk in his steps by knowing our God-given vision and following it. He said:

"For the Son of man is come to seek and to save that which was lost." [Luke 19: 10, John 10:10]

8. Your Vision Is Your Future

You need to write down the vision God has given you.

9. A Vision Serves As A Compass

As big as ocean liners are, and as expansive as the oceans are, the one instrument the captain of a ship cannot do without is a compass.

"The steps of a good man are ordered by the Lord: and he delighteth in his way." [Proverbs 37: 23]

10. A Vision Helps You Focus Your Energy

Many people would be glad just to know what the vision for their lives is, so that they can focus on it early. How many wasted dreams, wasted lives, because people have pursued what was not God's plan for their life.

> *"For I know the thoughts that I think toward you, saith the Lord, thoughts of peace, and not of evil, to give you an expected end."* [Jeremiah 29: 11]

11. A Vision Helps You Stay Within Your Gift Combination

It is not unusual to see people trying to be salesmen who do not have good communication skills, or the ability to persuade people to buy. When you begin to write your vision, if it is from God, it will confirm the gift or ability deposited in you and the things you desire to do.

12. Your Vision Will See You Through Tough Times

A vision is like a two-edged sword. It is both something to live or die for. As Joseph stood in front of his brothers stripped of his dream clothes, jeered at and mobbed; we do not know what he went through. This experience certainly did not tally with his dream of success and dominion. He probably did not realise that:

The wells of joy are dug sometimes with the spade of sorrow.

"They that sow in tears shall reap in joy. He that goeth forth and weepeth, bearing precious seed, shall doubtless come again with rejoicing, bringing his sheaves with him." [Psalm 126: 5-6]

13. Your Vision will Give You Hope

Satan may steal anything from you but do not let him steal your hope.

14. A Vision Is Something To Work With

A written vision is like raw material from which to chip out your dreams and aspirations. A man who has no dream, has no wings. He cannot fly. The only thing that sustained Joseph during thirteen years of non-stop humiliation was the dream in his heart.

15. A Vision Gives You A Defined Destination

All tickets carry on them a defined destination. Tickets bought are always time based. The traveller knows by the ticket in his hands when and where he will arrive. Your vision is your ticket to take you to God's original purpose for your life. If you do not find the vision you will jump on to the plane and will alight with others even if it is not where you are going.

> "I have fought a good fight. I have finished my course. I have kept the faith." [2 Timothy 4:7]

16. A Written Vision Will Make You Live A Selective Life

Vision makes your life unique. As I said earlier, while there may be things that are essences of all humans, there will be some things inherent in your vision that make you unique. Vision is personal.

17. Vision helps your perception of yourself and the future

He who never walks, except where he sees other peoples footprints, will make no discoveries.

18. A Vision Needs To Be Defined, Acquired And Applied

Your vision becomes effective in life, if you are able to define it in a manner that you can understand. You acquire your vision, first by praying to the Lord to make His mind known to you.

> "And Jabez was more honourable than his brethren: and his mother called his name Jabez, saying, Because I bare him with sorrow. And Jabez called on the God of Israel saying, Oh that thou wouldest bless me indeed, and enlarge my coast, and that thine hand might be with me, and that thou wouldest keep me from evil, that it may not grieve me! And God granted him that which he requested." [1 Chronicles 4: 9-10]

19. Vision Fuels Your Belief System

> "Looking unto Jesus the author and finisher of our faith; who for the joy that was set before him endured the cross, despising the shame, and is set down at the right hand of the throne of God." [Hebrews 12: 2]

20. Vision Is The Best Way To Measure Success

There are many well meaning men, women, ministries and businesses who are a success but feel like a failure because they did not define their vision. On the other hand are people who think they are successful, whereas they are achieving below their capacity.

17

Chapter Two

(12) "D's" OF PURPOSE

1. Dreams

The Bible says;

> *"For as a man thinketh in his heart so is he"*
> *[Proverbs 23: 7]*

Our thoughts govern so many areas of our life. People in their thought life who have accepted poverty find it difficult to break away from its hold. Dreams come in purposeful living, dreams are God given ideas. James Allen said '*Dreams are the saviours of mankind*', and Victor Hugo says, '*a timely idea and a thought is more than the military might of this world*'.

2. Design

Paul said:

> *"I press towards the mark for the prize of the high calling of God in Christ Jesus." [Philippians 3: 14]*

Paul had a clear blueprint of where he was going.

3. Decree

The Bible says when we give to God, windows of heaven will be open to us.

> *"See if I will not open you the windows of heaven an pour out a blessing that there shall not be room enough to receive it." [Malachi 3: 10]*

You must know how to decree it to come to pass. The ideas God sows into your heart, if unpursued, would become dormant. It is when you learn to decree that things start to come to pass. The Bible says, *'Concerning the work of my hand command ye me'.*

4. Discipline

It is important for you to realise that discipline is needed to live a life with a purpose because you are surrounded by people who are complacent about succeeding, as they have failed many times. Probably only five per cent of any nation's population really strives to maximize the abilities they have and become a person God wants them to be. In writing to Timothy, Paul said;

"But refuse profane and old wives fables and exercise thyself rather unto godliness."   [1 Timothy 4: 7]

5.   Determination

"But Daniel purposed in his heart that he would not defile himself with the portion of the king's meat, not with the wine which he drank: therefore, he requested of the prince of the eunuchs that he might not defile himself."
[Daniel 1: 8]

Without determination you would settle for temporary success and not realise that the enemy of the best is the good. Determination keeps you on track when things want to distract you from the purpose of God for your life. After all God must call you according to His purpose. He has a purpose.

"And we know that all things work together for good to them that love God, to them who are the called according to his purpose." [Romans 8: 28]

6.   Demonstration

It is not enough to discover that purpose gives meaning and direction to your life. It is important to demonstrate, even when you do not get encouragement, above your convictions.

"Wherefore by their fruits ye shall know them."[Matthew 7: 20]

7. Diligence

The Bible says,

> *"But the soul of the diligent shall be made fat."*
> *[Proverbs 13: 4]*

Diligence will spark fire in your life and make you truly live a life with a purpose.

After Abraham comes Isaac. He was also diligent in his work. The scripture says;

> *"In farming he tilled the land. And there was a famine in the land, beside the first famine that was in the days of Abraham. And Isaac went unto Abimelech King of the Philistines unto Gerar. Then Isaac sowed in that land, and received in the same year an hundredfold: and the Lord blessed him. And the man waxed great, and went forward, and grew until he became very great for he had possession of flocks and possession of herds, and great store of servants: and the Philistines envied him."*
> *[Genesis 26: 12-14]*

He must have been derided and laughed at when he tilled the land. In the time of farming he knew that he had activated God's promise by playing his own part and while everyone was busy laughing at Isaac, the scripture says he received a hundredfold. Sometimes when you sow seed into a ministry, when you discover a purpose in a prayerful life, or a life of consecration, the Philistines will mock you, but when the hundredfold return comes, you get various kinds of responses. A diligent man will wax great, will make progress. He will grow in many areas of his life, and will become exceedingly great.

A lazy Christian will live perpetually with poverty and lack. Purpose is seen in the life of Joseph, although he was sold to slavery by his brothers, because he was a man with a dream. The Bible says, *"he went about doing his business"*.

If you have no job create one. Inside you is the ability of God to bring to pass great and marvellous things, but you may never discover the highest height God wants you to rise to. From slavery the next step back in Joseph's life was imprisonment, and even there diligence made way for him. After interpreting the dream of the Pharaoh he became the diligent Prime Minister of the nation. *"By the blessing of the upright the city is exalted."*

> *"There is he that scattereth and yet increaseth; and there is that which holdeth more than is meet but it endeth to poverty."*

Understand that the diligent and the upright will be exalted and satisfied, while the lazy and the slothful who live by the law of average shall be put to forced labour by the state of the nation's economy.

Job was diligent. The Bible called him 'the greatest man in all the east'. God was so proud of Job that

He said to the devil, *'have you considered my servant Job?'* God wants you to make a purpose of your life, He wants to take the riches of the wicked and hand them over to the righteous, but even then only the diligent will enjoy it. The Bible says, *'let him who does not work not eat'.* If you walk in obedience and the laws of abundance, you will enjoy the inflow of divine ideas which will bring divine results.

8. Depend

> *"Trust in the Lord with all thine heart: and lean not unto thine own understanding. In all thy ways acknowledge him and he shall direct thy paths. Be not wise in thine own eyes: fear the Lord, and depart from evil, it shall be health to thy substance and with the first fruits of all thine increase: So shall thy barns be filled with plenty and thy presses shall burst out with new wine."*
> *[Proverbs 3: 5-10]*

Solomon said, *'trust in the Lord with all your heart'.* Have absolute confidence in Him. The word trust in Hebrew is *'batach'* meaning to attach oneself to, confide in, feel safe, secure, to be carefree and sometimes it means to rely on. It is a hope that is confident and an expectation, not a constant anxiety.

9. Disciple

Somebody somewhere is watching, duplicating what

you are doing. Jesus communicated the gospel and the purpose of His kingdom to twelve men, but two thousand years on the message is still the same. Disciple others to a life of purpose. You will discover many people who will come back and say *'thanks'*.

10. Duplicate

Duplicate your ideas by teaching them to others. Help your spouse to discover purpose. Help your children to discover purpose. Discover seminar studies, Bible teachings or books that can help people to take a giant leap and come out of the doldrums to run with the vision.

11. Delegate

> *"And the things that thou hast heard of me among many witnesses, the same commit thou to faithful men, who shall be able to teach others also."* [2 Timothy 2: 2]

12. Disappear

After helping people to discover purpose, do not hang around them too long. You might not help them much if you do not let them go out and be the person God wants them to be. It is good for them to model themselves after you initially, but the time has got to come when you must decrease and they shall increase.

Chapter Three

(6) WAYS TO HANDLE OPPORTUNITIES

"Brethren I count not myself to have apprehended: but this one thing I do, forgetting those things which are behind and reaching forth unto those things which are before. I press toward the mark for the prize of the high calling of God in Christ Jesus." [Philippians 3: 13-14]

Opportunities are unexpected doors which open for people. As in the case of Joseph, the Bible says, 'the Lord showed him mercy and gave him favour in the sight of the keeper of the prison'.

When he was sold to slavery, opportunities came by way of being exalted in the house of Potiphar, when he was thrown into prison and was forgotten. The opportunities came by the way God touched the prison keeper, who even made Joseph the head of all the prisoners. When Joseph was forgotten in prison by the King's Butler, God put a dream in Pharaoh's heart which was to be interpreted by Joseph.

1. Expect Opportunities

Be on alert for opportunities and open doors. The expectation of opportunities is expressed in words of Solomon,

> *"So shall you find favour and good understanding in the sight of God and man."* *[Proverbs 3: 4]*

2. Prospect Opportunities

To prospect opportunities you need to bloom where you are planted. You are independent. Do not conserve your energy when you serve people. They might not appreciate it, but as you bloom where you are planted, the beauty of your ability will attract others to you. It takes one person who believes in you to expose your ability to the world.

3. Respect Opportunities

Treat ideas reverently when they come, when doors open for you; do not take them for granted. The chance to work in any office, to speak, to represent may open or close other doors. In writing to Timothy, Paul said;

> *"For they that have used the office of a deacon well purchase to themselves a good degree, and great boldness in the faith which is in Christ Jesus." [1 Timothy 3: 13]*

Jesus also said;

> *"Give not that which is holy unto the dogs, neither cast ye your pearls before swine lest they trample them under their feet and turn again and rend you." [Matthew 7: 6]*

How many people have been given the opportunity to serve in some great position, but they did not make good use of this opportunity and they missed out?

4. Inspect opportunities

It is an early step to earning self-respect and self-respect starts when you start inspecting your own ideas. Do not put down your God-given ideas. They may not be as lofty as the man next door. They may not sound profound, but by the time you put them together and present them to others, because they burned in your heart, if you follow them through, they will bless you and others.

5. Select opportunities

It is important for you to realise that where you end up is not as important as what you learn along the way. One of your strategies for taking charge of opportunities is to actually analyse some of them as they come.

Select the ones you want to devote your time to.
Some of them come in disguise of difficulties.
Diamonds are never beautiful when they are initially
picked up. They are hard, unattractive pieces of
stone. The beauty never comes as the rough edges
are being chipped.

6. Protect opportunities

Solomon said;

> *"Yet a little sleep, a little slumber, a little folding of the
> hands to sleep."* *[Proverbs 6: 10]*

Many people have lost the chance of being blessed,
the chance of promotion, spiritual well-being,
enjoying their marriage and a healthy life because
they procrastinate on everything. They will not do
much, because tomorrow is always there; they will
not go for the next job because they have the best
and the enemy of best is good.

Chapter Four

(15) BLESSINGS OF DIVINE WISDOM

1. You Will Understand the Importance of Reverence for God

"Then shalt thou understand the fear of the Lord, and find the knowledge of God." [Proverb 2:5]

2. Divine Wisdom Produces Knowledge

"Then shalt thou understand the fear of the Lord, and find the knowledge of God." [Proverb 2: 5]

3. Long Life

"To deliver thee from the strange woman, even from the stranger which flattereth with her words;" [Proverb 2: 16]

"Hear, O my son, and receive my sayings; and the years of thy life shall be many." [Proverb 4: 10]

"For whoso findeth me findeth life, and shall obtain favour of the Lord." [Proverb 8: 35]

4. Wealth

"Length of days is in her right hand; and in her left hand riches and honour." [Proverb 3: 16]

5. Vitality

"So shall they be life unto thy soul, and grace to thy neck." [Proverb 3: 22]

6. Protection from falling

"Then shalt thou walk in thy way safely, and thy foot shall not stumble." [Proverb 3: 23]

7. Safety in all your ways

"Then shalt thou walk in thy way safely, and thy foot shall not stumble." [Proverb 3: 23]

8. Fear-Free

"When thou liest down, thou shall not be afraid: yea, thou shalt lie down, and thy sleep shall be sweet." [Proverbs 3: 24]

9. Rest

"When thou liest down, thou shall not be afraid: yea, thou shalt lie down, and thy sleep shall be sweet."
[Proverbs 3: 24]

10. You will Inherit Honour, Glory, Esteem

"Exalt her, and she shall promote thee: she shall bring thee to honour, when thou dost embrace her."
[Proverb 4: 8]

11. Cherishing Wisdom Results in Promotion

"Exalt her, and she shall promote thee: she shall bring thee to honour, when thou dost embrace her."
[Proverb 4: 8]

12. Honour

"Exalt her, and she shall promote thee: she shall bring thee to honour, when thou dost embrace her."
[Proverb 4: 8]

13. Dressed with Grace and Crowned with Glory

"She shall give to thine head an ornament of grace: a crown of glory shall she deliver to thee." *[Proverb 4: 9]*

14. You will be Preserved and Guarded Jealously by the Lord

"Forsake her not, and she shall preserve thee: love her, and she shall keep thee." [Proverb 4: 6]

15. Direction

"But the path of the just is as the shining light, that shineth more and more unto the perfect day." [Proverb 4: 18]

Chapter Five

(20) MANIFESTATIONS OF DIVINE SUCCESS

1. An Excellent Spirit

"Forasmuch as an excellent spirit, and knowledge, and understanding, interpreting of dreams, and shewing of hard sentence, and dissolving of doubts, were found in the same Daniel, whom the king named Belteshazzar: now let Daniell be called, and he will shew the interpretation." [Daniel 5: 12]

2. Integrity

"Let integrity and uprightness preserve me; for I wait on thee." [Psalm 25: 21]

3. Physical Health And Healing

"And said, If thou wilt diligently hearken to the voice of

*the Lord thy God, and wilt do that which is right in his
sight, and wilt give ear to his commandments, and keep
all his statutes. I will put none of these diseases upon
thee, which I have brought upon the Egyptians: for I am
the Lord that healeth thee." [Exodus 15: 26]*

4. Kingdom Consciousness

*"But seek ye first the kingdom of God, and his
righteousness; and all these things shall be added unto
you." [Matthew 6: 33]*

5. Faithful Stewardship

*"And the Lord said, Who then is that faithful and wise
steward, whom his lord shall make ruler over his
household, to give them their portion of meat in due
season?" [Luke 12: 42]*

6. Financial Blessing

*"Beloved, I wish above all thing that thou mayest prosper
and be in health, even as thy soul prospereth."
[III John 2]*

7. Spiritual Progress

*"But grow in grace, and in the knowledge of our Lord
and Saviour Jesus Christ. To him be glory both now and
for ever. Amen." [II Peter 3: 18]*

8. Consistent Prayer Life

*"Praying always with all prayer and supplications in the
Spirit, and watchin thereunto with all perseverence and*

supplication for all saints;" [Ephesians 6: 18]

9. Focus

"Brethren, I count not myself to have apprehended: but this one thing I do, forgetting those things which are behind, and reaching forth unto those things which are before." [Philippians 3: 13]

10. Delight In God's Word

"Blessed is the man that walketh not in the counsel of the ungodly, nor standeth in the way of sinners, nor sitteth in the seat of the scornful." [Psalm 1: 1-2]

11. Favour

"Thou shalt arise, and have mercy upon Zion: for the time to favour her, yea, the set time, is come." [Psalm 102: 13]

12. Sense of Purpose

"In whom also we have obtained and inheritance, being predestined according to the purpose of him who worketh all things after the counsel of his own will:" [Ephesians 1:11]

13. Clear Purpose

"If a man die, shall he live again? All the days of my appointed time will I wait, till my change come." [Job 14: 14]

14. Divine Elevation

"He raiseth up the poor out of the dust, and lifteth the needy out of the dounghill;

That he may set him with princes, even with the princes of his people.

He maketh the barren woman to keep house, and to be a joyful mother of children. Praise ye the Lord."
[Psalm 113: 7-9]

15. Change of Circumstance

"And the Lord turned the captivity of Job, when he prayed for his friends: also the Lord gave Job twice as much as he had before." [Job 42: 10]

16. Anointing

"And it shall come to pass in that day, that his burden shall be taken away from off thy shoulder, and his yoke from off thy neck, and the yoke shall be distroyed because of the anointing." [Isaiah 10: 27]

17. Breakthrough

"And David came to Baal-perazim, and David smote them there, and said, The Lord hath broken forth upon mine enemies before me, as the breach of waters. Therefore he called the name of that place Baal-perazim."
[II Samuel 5: 20]

18. Clarity of Vision

"And the Lord answered me, and said, Write the vision,

and make it plain upon tables, that he may run that readeth it." *[Habakkuk 2: 2]*

19. Renewed Mind

"I beseech you therefore, brethren by the mercies of God, that ye present your bodies a living sacrifice, holy, acceptable onto God, which is your reasonable service.

And be not conformed to this world: but be ye transformed by the renewing of your mind, that ye may prove what is that ye may prove what is that good, and acceptable, and perfect, will of God." [Romans 12: 1-2]

20. Finishing Well

"I have fought a good fight, I have finished my course, I have kept the faith:" [2 Timothy 4:7]

Chapter Six

8 WAYS TO SET GOALS FOR LIFE

S *pecific*
M *easureable*
A *achievable*
R *realistic*
T *ime-Based*

O *n-paper*
N *otable*
E *xciting*

1. Specific

"Brethren, I count not myself to have apprehended: but this one thing I do, forgetting those things which are behind, and reaching forth unto those things which are before." [Philippians 3: 13]

2. Measurable

"I press towards the mark for the prize of the high calling of God in Christ Jesus." [Philippians 3: 14]

3. Achievable

"I can do all things through Christ which strengtheneth me." [Philippians 4: 13]

4. Realistic

"For I say, through the grace given unto me, to every man that is among you, not to think of himself more highly than he ought to think; but to think soberly, accordingg as God hath dealt to every man the measure of faith." [Romans 12: 3]

5. Time-Based

"For the vision is yet for an appointed time, but at the end it shall speak, and not lie: though it tarry, wait for it; because it will surely come, it will not tarry." [Habakkuk 2: 3]

6. On-Paper

"And the Lord answered me, and said, Write the vision, and make it plain upon tables, that he may run that readeth it." [Habakkuk 2: 2]

7. Notable

"The secret things belong unto the Lord our God: but those things which are revealed belong unto us and to our children for ever, that we may do all the words of this law." [Deuteronomy 29: 29]

8. Exciting

"Where there is no vision, the people perish: but he that keepeth the law, happy is he." {Proverb 29:18]

Chapter Seven

⑤ WAYS TO PURSUE YOUR DREAMS

"And when his brethren saw that their father loved hem more than all his brethren, they hated him, and could not speak peaceably unto him. And Joseph dreamed a dream and he told it to his brethren: and they hated him yet more. And he said unto them, Hear, I pray you, this dream which I have dreamed:

For behold, we were binding sheaves in the field, and, lo, my sheaf arose, and also stood upright ; and, behold, your sheaves stood round about, and made obeisance to my sheaf. And his brethren, said to him, Shalt thou indeed have dominion over us? And they hated him yet the more for his dreams, and for his words." [Genesis 37: 4-8]

Five words convey truths about the life of Joseph,

from the beginning of his dream to the fulfilment.
They are: Perceive, Believe, Conceive, Achieve and
Receive. These words also convey the steps you
need to take in fulfilling your God-given vision.
They may be taken all at once or step by step, but
the intention is that you achieve God's original
purpose for your life.

1. Perceive

The word perception in the Hebrew is *'yada'*. It
carries various meanings:

*To know properly, ascertain by seeing, observe, care,
recognise, acknowledge, acquaint, aware,
comprehend, to discover, make to know, or come to a
place of knowing.*

In the Greek, it comes from the word *'theoreo'*. It
carries the meaning:

Discern, Behold, Consider or look at.

God's perception is demonstrated in calling forth a
perfectly ordered universe, which should have taken
millions of years to create, but which He created in
six days.

His perception is revealed as:

➢   He looked at a shepherd boy - David and He

saw a King. That is perception.

> He looked at a murderer - Moses and He saw a deliverer. That is perception.

> He looked at a slave called Daniel and He saw a leader. That is perception.

> He looked at Abram whose name meant 'father' and at ninety-nine was still childless and called him Abraham which means 'The Father of Nations'. God was not looking at Abraham's present state, He was looking at Abraham's future. That is perception.

2. Believe

There are times we come in contact with people who do not believe in our visions and dreams. Some do not stop there, they express their hatred or disapproval. Some go further and try to frustrate our dream. In pursuance of their hatred, the brothers of Joseph tried to bury the dreamer. They thought if the dreamer was buried, his dream would be gone.

> *"And all his sons and all his daughters rose up to comfort him; and he said, For I will go down into the grave unto my son mourning. Thus his father wept for him."*
> *[Genesis 37: 35]*

3. Conceive

Conceiving is the mid-point from what you perceive as your God-given vision and dream to what you will eventually receive.

Almost every instance where the work 'conceive' was used with reference to thought or idea, in Scripture has to do with thoughts of evil. It is a shocking revelation to see such a powerful tool of breakthrough like conceiving being negatively used. For example Job's friend said;

> "They conceive mischief, and bring forth vanity, and their belly prepareth deceit." [Job 15: 35]

4. Achieve

The whole purpose of this book is for you to find your God-given vision and dream and to fulfil it. Wealth would be meaningless if all we want to do is to show how much we own. Glorying in poverty would also be wrong if all it does for us is to provide a source of escape from dreaming and catching the vision of God for our lives.

The next step is for us to achieve our God-given vision. Achievement is simply another way of saying work.

5. Receive

In Luke chapter 5, Peter encountered the power of the Lord Jesus to turn a meaningless life into one full of visions and dreams.

> *"... Launch out into the deep, and let down you nets for a draught. And Simon answering said unto him, Master, we have toiled all the night, and have taken nothing: nevertheless at thy word I will let down the net. And when they had this done, they enclosed a great multitude of fishes: and their net brake." [Luke 5: 4-6]*

Chapter Eight

(10) DREAM KILLERS

Dream takers basically are states of our own emotional experiences which we may have had, which can freeze the dreams and aspirations God has put in our hearts to achieve. I have listed the following:

Dream haters, complacency, fear, tradition, mediocrity, short term thinking, fatigue and doubt.

If dreams are God's original intention for our lives, if they are the compass to guide us from wasting our time on this planet, then we will do everything to acquire the vision and dream God has for us.

Let us look at these dream takers one by one. As you read, if you are held in the trap of any of them, make a quality decision and shake it off in the name of the Lord.

1. Dream Haters

Every dreamer attracts dream haters. There is a lot of similarity between Joseph and Daniel. Both were sold to slavery, interpreted dreams of Kings, had dreams and became Prime Ministers. they also shared a similarity of having dream haters. The moment Joseph announced his dreams and visions, he provoked the envy and hatred of his brothers.

> "And Joseph dreamed a dream, and he told it his brethren: and they hated him yet the more." [Genesis 37: 5]

> "And his brethren envied him; but his father observed the saying:" [Genesis 37: 11]

Whenever you announce your vision of evangelism, building the kingdom of God, reaching more souls for Jesus, and ministering to the sick, demonic dream haters will be put into action by the enemy.

His brothers envied him. This brings out the truth that two or three years after a person is born again, his circle of social contacts are essentially believers. If he suffers and it hurt it is not likely to be from unbelievers. The second major dream hater he encountered was Potiphar's wife. Her action brings to remembrance Proverbs 6: 26;

> "For by means of a whorish woman, a man is brought to a piece of bread: and the adulteress will hunt for the precious life." [Proverbs 6: 26]

Following his experience in the house of Potiphar, he now finds himself in prison. Potiphar forgot all the young man's previous good deeds. We do not know if he put Joseph in the king's prison because he did not believe his wife. In the sight of men all the good deeds we may have done are wiped away in one day by one mistake, or false evil report which may have no proof or foundation.

Having interpreted the dream of the Chief Baker and the Butler, Joseph had confidence in the promise of the Chief Butler to help him, when he was out of prison. But the Bible says:

> *"Yet did not the chief butler remember Joseph; but forgot him." [Genesis 40: 23]*

When we put our confidence in man, close friends, associates or relations they may disappoint us. Throughout the Bible we are only instructed to love man and trust God. There is no place in scripture where we are told to trust in man.

One of the dream haters that could destroy a person's future is putting his confidence in the wrong place.

2. Complacency

'It does not matter what we do, God will bless our efforts.' This kind of statement is a prognosis of ministries, ministers and life of believers who want to settle for the enemy called average. You cannot be an average Christian and receive a full time reward. God cares what we do with our time and how we live our lives here.

If He does not care, He would not have given you the vision and dreams that had crossed your heart at one time or the other, which you probably refused to pursue because you were unsure if they were from Him.

3. Fear

The simplest way to define fear is:

> **F**alse
> **E**vidence
> **A**ppearing
> **R**eal

Can you imagine if Joseph's dream had been frustrated by a haranguing fear instilled by his father, brothers, Potiphar experience, or his own presumption?

Many do not dream any new dream because the previous dreams they had never materialised or when they shared it with someone their sixteen feet dream was reduced to six feet.

There are people who are afraid of failure and people who are afraid of succeeding because they know success attracts criticism.

4. Tradition

'This is the way I have always done it and it has always worked for me. Why do I need to change?'

Tradition is a very strong blockade to dreaming a new dream. It is a clog in the wheel to fulfilling God's visions and dreams for us.

5. Mediocrity

Mediocrity is a dream taker and probably one of the worst. If you are mediocre you will be busy or engaged in fruitless programmes and not achieving your full potential. Mediocres like to be seen to be busy. Busyness does not mean achievement. Many do not qualify what they are doing, to see how valuable it is to the fulfilling of their dreams and visions. If you have a plumber in a company, who takes two hours to fix a broken pipe, he is not mediocre, but if in the attempt to save £40:00, the Executive Director of the same company spends four hours of company time doing the same job, he would have wasted more money and quality time in a job he is unskilled to do as a highly paid executive.

6. Short-term Thinking

God's vision for your life is long-term and is intended to outlive your short-term thinking, as goals for your life extend into eternity. Ironically, when Joseph was about to die at one hundred and thirty years, he made the children of Israel swear that his bones would be buried in Canaan.

In the book of Hebrews, Chapter 11, where the roll call of those who lived by faith is stated, the outstanding thing recorded about Joseph was his instructions concerning his bones.

> *"By faith Joseph, when he died, made mention of the departing of the children of Israel; and gave commandment concerning his bones."*
> *[Hebrews 11: 22]*

The question is - what is so special about bones?

There is a lot.

Joseph foresaw the slavery, he saw the children of Israel give up God's long-time vision of settling in Canaan.

He therefore gave instructions that his vision must outlive him. The children of Israel must go back to Canaan. All through slavery in Egypt, for 430 years,

Joseph's instruction was one source of their motivation. It is almost like they were saying to each other, 'We must go back, we must carry Joseph's bones, there is still a place to reach, there is another land, there is a future'.

In your divine destiny, God has put enough in you to continue after your death. You are a blessing to your generation and the one to come.

7. Fatigue

There is a point when tiredness comes in and we lose a clear definition of our vision and our thrust. We lose the spiritual and mental agility for running with our God-given vision. Fatigue will try to twist your vision. The best thing to do at such a time is to wait on the Lord for a renewal of strength.

> *"But they that wait upon the Lord shall renew their strength: they shall mount up with wings as eagles; they shall run, and not be weary; and they shall walk, and not faint." [Isaiah 40: 31]*

8. Doubt

> *"And to whom sware he that they should not enter into his rest, but to them that believed not? So we see that they could not enter in because of unbelief."*
> *[Hebrews 3: 18-19]*

Doubt is the greatest thief of God's blessings. The

things God will manifest to your renewed heart will be more than you can perceive, but once you are able to perceive you need to believe. When you believe, you will be able to conceive them and achieve them. If you doubt, you limit God, because God has committed Himself to honour whatever is accompanied by faith.

9. Stagnation

Stagnation may be the result if we do not remain in motion with our God-given idea. Many people get riveted to what they consider success now. Being hooked to the glory of yesterday's success could be a major deterrent to the greater potential we have. When people stagnate they join the mass majority who never achieve their God-given vision. As a matter of fact, most people operate only on ten per cent of their God-given ability.

10. Procrastination

'Procrastination' they say, is the thief of all time. The uncertainty of the future and the success we know from the past, easily deceives and makes people procrastinate on the steps which would have brought the fulfilment of God's vision for their life.

The physical blessing and progress of Lot in the city of Sodom made him hesitate when the angels of the

Lord came to take him out of imminent danger.

> *"And while he lingered, the men laid hold upon his hand and upon the hand of his wife and upon the hand of his two daughters: the Lord being merciful unto him: and they brought him forth and set him without the city."* [Genesis 19: 16]

Procrastination could also be a product of the uncertainties of the future but:

➤ if hunger is proof that food exists
➤ if thirst is proof that liquid or water exists
➤ desire is the proof that supply exists.

Chapter Nine

⑤ REASONS TO KEEP YOUR DREAMS ALIVE

An attempt to run our life without the hand of the Master will result in frustration and futility.

God's vision for your life is like a fingerprint or the structure of the human face. No one has the exact kind of fingerprint you have, and there are no two similar faces in the whole world.

1. Your vision is **that unique calling on your life which no one else can fulfil but you, in the whole of the economy of God.**

2. You need to keep your God-given dream alive because **you will only know true fulfilment in life when you discover what makes you**

unique in a sea of billions of people and you set out to achieve your divine destiny.

The desire to know divine destiny led to the frustrations of the Sixties from which songs which expressed man's feeling of being a speck in a vast universe were written.

In such a disillusioned state young men and women who did not know their God-given dream ended up trying everything to find fulfilment, that is Eastern religion, pot, LSD, etc.

3.   When you discover your God-given dream and keep it alive, **you will live a life which is authentic and not synthetic.** Like I often say when preaching, many people start their life as originals, they end it as body copies of photocopies. While it is great to learn from people whom you see as mentors, it is important to realise that there is something which makes you YOU.

4.   The reason for keeping your dream alive is that **it is your eye into the future.**

> *"While we look not at the things which are seen, but at the things which are not seen: for the things which are seen are temporal; but the things which are not seen are eternal." [2 Corinthians 4: 18]*

A man who lives his life guided by his five senses, who has not connection or relationship with the

Holy Spirit, will miss out on half of his life because there is a dimension to life which is spiritual. When God puts in our hearts visions, redemptive revelation or dreams, which He wants us to fulfil we will be restless until we reach forth into eternity and bring the things that are eternal into the physical.

5.   There is a fifth reason for keeping your vision alive and that is the fact that **God has an original intention for sending you to this planet.** A translation of Romans 8: 28 says:

> *"All things work together for good to them that love God. To them that are 'called according to His original intention.'"* [Strong's Hebrew Greek Dictionary]

This revelation should make you ask questions at this point.

> ➢   Am I in the centre of God's will?
> ➢   Am I following God's plan for my life?
> ➢   What is His original plan for may Life?
> ➢   Do I try to be somebody else?

Too many people are neutral when it comes to achieving God's purpose for their life. If they are salesmen, for example, they are not ready to do their business with the extra touch; they are not ready to work out doing the best for God. Keeping your dream alive will require doing more than 'just moving' but being *'at the right speed'.*

PETITIONING GOD IN PRAYER

NAME (MR & MRS, MR, MRS, MISS):
_____

ADDRESS:
_____

TOWN:
_____

COUNTY: _____ POST CODE: _____

PHONE (H): _____

    (W): _____

Let us join our faith with yours for your prayer needs, Fill out the space
below and send to the address given

YOUR PETITION

1. _____

2. _____

3. _____

4. _____

5. _____

6. _____

7. _____

8. _____

9. _____

10. _____

MAIL TO:-

Kingsway International Christian Centre

1 Darnley Road, Off Mare Street, Hackney, London, E9 6QH.

If you want prayer immediately, call HOPELINE on **0181 525 0000**

PERSONAL DETAILS

NAME (MR & MRS, MR, MRS, MISS): _____

ADDRESS: _____
_____

TOWN: _____

COUNTY: _____ POST CODE: _____

PHONE (H) _____
(W) _____

FOR YOUR INFORMATION

❑ Please send me your free quarterly magazine
KINGSWAY DIGEST,

❑ Please put me on your mailing list,

❑ Please send me a catalogue of Pastor Matthew's
tapes and books.

MAIL TO:-

Kingsway International Christian Centre

1 Darnley Road, Off Mare Street, Hackney, London, E9 6QH.

CLARICE:
THE VISITOR

a wave would be hear
to enfold the note
spraying its fo
music. I gr
my thing
struck
in

IDRA NOVEY

Clarice:
The Visitor

CENTER FOR WRITERS & TRANSLATORS
THE AMERICAN UNIVERSITY OF PARIS

—

SYLPH EDITIONS

In Edward Gorey's *The Doubtful Guest*, a penguin-like creature
arrives in a scarf and white sneakers and presses its face to the
wallpaper. In one of Gorey's drawings that accompany the text,
the inhabitants of the house cluster behind a curtain to observe
their curious guest. Later, the creature vanishes and turns up in
the kitchen inside a tureen. In the evening, the visitor tears pages
out of books, is subject to 'fits of bewildering wrath, / During
which it would hide all the towels from the bath'.

Guests can be like this, and yet what is the point of having a
home if you don't allow for the entry of other voices, of visitors
and the surprising shifts of mind they provoke, shifts which keep
you changing and thereby alive?

Every author I've translated has become this sort of visitor,
altering what I expect to find – or lose – in my living room, what
I put in – or take out – of my own writing. But no author's
voice has had such a profound effect on me as that of Brazilian
writer Clarice Lispector. While translating her novel *The Passion
According to G.H.*, I found she took up residence in my life with
such intensity that it was impossible to forget her breath-altering
sentences even as I was sitting down to eat with actual house-
guests in my home. A friend would arrive and I would hear his
speech in a peculiar way, with a heightened attention to the way
his sentences were structured, what his declarations spoke around
and against. Occasionally, I would hear my own voice as if it were
coming from across a room and have to make an effort to return
to my uninhabited self.

But what self was that, exactly? What does the visitation of an
author's voice do to your relationship with your own mind – mind
being the place where thoughts come and go but *mind* also being
a verb, meaning 'to be troubled by' as well as 'to obey'? What if
the intensity of what you're translating leaves you so stunned alive

you stand in your kitchen and can't make dinner, your author's company troubling you into considering the possibility of God?

One way I've found to scurry around such questions is to draft a poem or two on the matter. In the first sequence included here, I wrote each of the poems in conversation with a quotation from *Cartas perto do coração* (Letters Close to the Heart), a volume of correspondence made up of letters between Clarice Lispector and the Brazilian novelist Fernando Sabino when Lispector was living abroad as a new mother and diplomat's wife.

In the second sequence, Lispector's presence is less overt, although there is an appearance from the slow-dying cockroach whose steady stare causes a metaphysical crisis for the narrator in *The Passion According to G.H.* For months, I felt the possibility of that cockroach as I matched my son's tiny socks or filled pots of coffee for the guests who kept arriving to meet him. Would the roach emerge while my sister-in-law and her husband were sleeping on my pull-out couch, or to greet the friend from college who kept looking away?

The entrance of a guest scrambles the syntax of daily life. As in Gorey's book, it is only a matter of time before a new presence in the house makes a person turn and see her carefully selected pictures 'askew on their hooks'.

Idra Novey

Letters to C

I

'At three in the afternoon, I'm the
most demanding woman in the
world...When it's over, six in the
afternoon comes, also indescribable, in
which I turn blind.'

Lispector to Fernando Sabino, 1946

Dear C, I'm turning from.
Have been syntaxed and stirred into a purple.
Blurred to blind.
I made a mess of page twenty-two,
couldn't resurrect what you left unsaid
into words that wouldn't.
Do you believe in grieving?
I mean for language, the endangered
animal of, fleeing into caves.
I can only keep after it in fits
or I get trapped
in the keeping after. That,
and bliss.
Your spinning but devoted
I.N.

II

'*The word that's missing in order to complete
a thought may take half a lifetime to appear.*'

Lispector to Fernando Sabino, 1953

I've vanished
from waiting for the word that will.

The way my neighbor
backs up his car so fast he hits the trash bags

and they bury him.
And so is living for me, in the mis-appeared.

In the clear that will not,
Clarice. Your meanings lean like buildings

in the wind from.
You worked as a translator, know one has to hang

the missing word
like a hat on a wall without a hook.

I'm either the hook
that could have or the hat which has to.

Falling now.

III

'I know I'm using words that perhaps sound too
strong (I had a night of insomnia, believe me...)'
Lispector to Fernando Sabino, 1957

C, I dropped your sequence

in hot water. I talked
to the boil. I said Here

is my thumb for you to burn.

Here is the soft heart
of my hand and my arm and

the nape of my wreck.

I said vapor, just take me.
I'm done burning

with these pages. Being invisible

doesn't mean a person
won't blister, doesn't mean

the blisters won't fill

with pockets of water
or when lanced the rawest flesh

won't emerge. First the word

then the murky leak begins – what
other minds may press against

but never skin.

IV

'Here the cold is starting, which
without meaning to, changes our lives.'

Lispector to Fernando Sabino, 1956

Down into
the night of it,
the blight of a word
from a dark farm
which may fog
continuously.

Down to
the symbol of it
and wondering
at five a.m. if
it's the winter
in translation
that makes people
distrust it, these dust-hours
of doubting.

Down again
to the hesitation
which may (or
may not) turn
into the stamen
of a flower – stamen loose
from the Greek
for man's house
and now
there's that lodge.

Down then
to etymology.
Or back to filament.
To flowering.
Up all night.

V

*'Fernando, this is a ghost
named Clarice writing to you.'*

Lispector to Fernando Sabino, 1956

Dear author ghost,
dear desk, I've left you
for a man. The body
has its callings
after all.

Your mortal
but abiding

I.N.

VI

*'I'm working badly and badly on a
romance or novel, struggling against
a very true impression of futility.'*

Lispector to Fernando Sabino, 1954

Dear C,
feeling stuck today,
luckless, the puckered skin
around a scar.

At a luncheon,
a man tucked up to say
translation was once
considered women's work, did
I know it, lowly
as literary dishwashing.

Alchemy, too, I told him,
was seen once
as mere cooking
with gold.

It grows so old,
the effort of diplomacy.
Did you ever
imagine vanishing
behind a giant
Chinese fan?

I picture the fan
covered with hundreds
of flying oven mitts,
a dozen winged iron pans.

All of them soaring – airborne
as women
after centuries deferred.

VII

'...in a small daily life, in which a person risks herself
more deeply, with greater threats.'

Lispector to Fernando Sabino, 1953

If a woman translates a woman writes a woman who sculpts a
pleasant something out of clumps of bread.

If the clatter of earrings.

If the clumps become less pleasant, can no longer be called the tender
rendering of bread.

If a woman translates a woman writes a woman who is less and less.

If the flesh of bread.

If pressed between fingers and folded.

If the word for rolling, for oratorio and deadline.

If collapsing beside.

If collapsing under.

If the subtle clatter of earrings is.

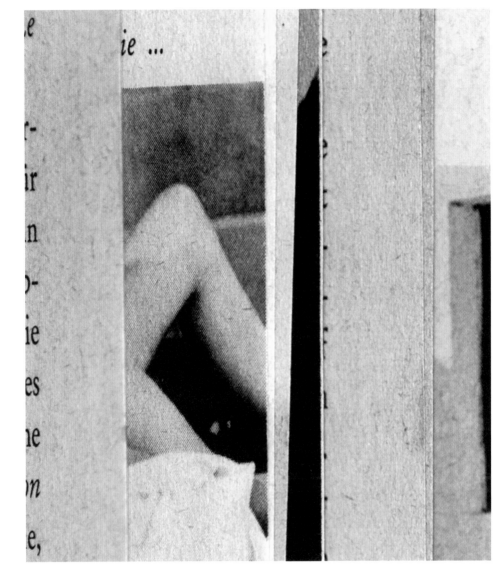

VIII

C, I can't recall
who I was before the haunting handiwork
of translating you.

When the man at the store said, Miss,
you are dripping with it,
I thought he meant your novel.

And the unanswerables.
The false sanity of fancy language.

What was I failing at
before this – and why is it
failure makes a person feel
so irremediably alive?

This blue work.
This gluing of impossibilities.

Olhando ainda. Still looking.
Looking, still.

IX

'...this is a letter for sharing news and complaints.'
Lispector to Fernando Sabino, 1953

These letters, C,
are my geese to you.
They come backward
in the formation of a letter
from an alphabet
that can only be flown.

So much geese-work
leaves me fat and baffled,
my vocabulary slack
with Latinates.

I miss my sleek years, slender
with the certainty of what I knew.
What's terrifying about you, C,
is that you know
what you don't know, what
none of us do.

But I have to go – my sons
want me to speak in puppet.
So it is performing your words:
I'm a blue-faced creature
with seams between her fingers.
A being with no eyelids
who can bow but cannot blink.

X

' . . . it's so hard to leave the routine of this house.'

Lispector to Fernando Sabino, 1957

I know all the frozen fish involved
in leaving a house. I know the fossils,
the upholstered impossibles.

    For your green noon, C,

I tried to play the ballad
as you had it, crisply enough
to cut the strings of the balloon

    then cut the sky

into which such balloons
rise as fugitives.

    Your choosing green

for midday seemed
deeply blue to me. I heard
the unsaid color in it,

    the thrum of moving darkly

along the brightness
of a house, the high of a word
in that silence.

XI

A fantasy:

We are standing by a sandbox,
both lost
in the camouflage of those hours,

their boxes.

I ask about the pronoun you often place
before God.

You go on smoking.

The sun now
above the playground begins to burn

then
the snow burns. My sons are grown.

At last
you turn to answer and I

am listening.

Regarding Marmalade,
Cognates, and Visitors

July

V arrives, expects nothing
but to witness our lives and find kindness
and why shouldn't she
but for the boiling water my partner spills
on my arm and the FUCK'S SAKE
that escapes my mouth now the snout
of the spitting mammal in me.
If there's a craft to the failing of simple
expectations, I have mastered it
and majestically – but if there's something
that must be said, it must be said,
Lispector says of a woman entering
an empty room and finding a version
of herself so dark it makes her pause
and really see it, how she's no better
than the cockroach in her closet
so she eats it.

August

O looks totaled,
older but more wholly
himself as we kiss in the tradition
of his country, where he kissed
a man recently and told
his wife, and things ended,
this man who bends now
to kiss my infant son
after which we have nothing
to say – our particles the same,
so much else altered
or halting. We log the hours
till he asks about my sadness
in his country, how it lasted,
how it left, and I tell him
it was the brown-yellow
of dead grass on a hill
until the hill was gone.

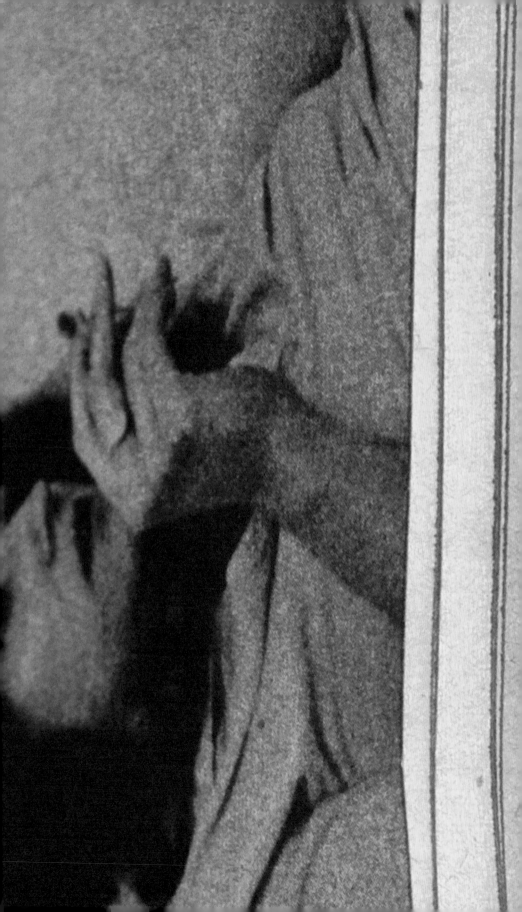

(On the Divine as Absence in) October

If our view were not a Holiday Inn
but a fringe of trees, I could say, G, here
is our greenly hidden.
                            If we lived
amid Joe-Pye weed and high grass
instead of spackle and peeling plaster
I could say perhaps
                            I'm listening to G now
but mean the owl, a wind playing the silo,
a sticking sorrow,
                            any sound but the snore
of our latest visitor on the futon. Dear G,
please make him turn, make me kinder.
I'm not far from unfathoming it all.

November

To choose not to know:
the option.
           But there was

a small plastic device
that offered it,
           the whole knowing

in no more than a minute.
An instant
           translation of

what was splitting
into cells
           or wasn't.

I simply had to close
a door, bend
           over a device.

Dear S had arrived
to stand with me
           in the after

the two of us still
as clay pots
           holding the knowledge

my body had begun
or would not.

December

F texts through breakfast, texts
through dinner, texts stepping in
and out of the bathroom, a towel
on his head. Texts as we talk
about literature and he zippers
his compact black valise, says Idra,
querida, never seen you
look better.

December, Still

The last bees have gone.
The quiet in my hive is

of wind licking a vacant house.
I am the vagrant inside, staking out

where to place my few thoughts
and boots. If I ought

to start a fire, let it undo
the living room.

January

Three days after A leaves, I see him still.
Still naked in the kitchen, still gazing
at the holiday cards on the fridge.
I cower again, he covers his penis,
the season goes on.

March

Something's gone and spilled
in our speakers, or why else
does M sound this rubbed out –
her voice metallic and skittering,
static
      then absent.

We get up from the couch,
sit back down, switch to Spanish,
mumble in English, nothing intelligible
but that
she has been.

April

Does no dishes, dribbles sauce
across the floor. Is more dragon
than spaniel, more flammable
than fluid. Is the loosening
in the knit of me, the mixed-fruit
marmalade in the kitchen of me.
Wakes my disco and inner hibiscus,
the Hector in the ever-mess of my Troy.
All wet mattress to my analysis,
he's stayed the loudest and longest
of any houseguest, is calling now
as I write this, tiny B who brings the joy.

June

I serve J a plate she doesn't take,
offer her a softer chair. We were close
as cognates once, nearly holy
to one another – which comes down now
to coming down
to what?
                    To having been cognates once.
Swappable as the *agua* my son says
for the sky in his tiny Find-the-World books.
And we find it, the same blue.

COLOPHON

THE CAHIERS SERIES · NUMBER 23
ISBN: 978-1-909631-07-6

Printed by Principal Colour, Paddock Wood, on
Neptune Unique (text) and Chagall (dust jacket).
Set in Giovanni Mardersteig's Monotype Dante.

Series Editor: Dan Gunn
Associate Series Editor: Daniel Medin
Design: Sylph Editions Design

Text: ©Idra Novey, 2014
Images: © Erica Baum, 2014

Grateful acknowledgment to *Poetry* and *Asymptote*,
where some of these poems first appeared.

CENTER FOR WRITERS & TRANSLATORS
THE AMERICAN UNIVERSITY OF PARIS

SYLPH EDITIONS, LONDON | 2014

www.aup.edu · www.sylpheditions.com

there will be now
not to finish
the point?
long as
know
it

in my mouth.
ended. I am
there one
I knew
wise